Hardcover ISBN: 978-0-9930881-3-1

Published On: 1 September 2017
Copyright (c) Neuri Consulting LLP

Author: Gojko Adzic
Copy-editor: Mary White (www.writeclick.co.uk)
Illustrator: Nikola Korac

Published by:
Neuri Consulting LLP
25 Southampton Buildings
London WC2A 1AL
United Kingdom

For information on bulk purchases and translation rights, please write to *contact@neuri.co.uk*.

HUMANS vs COMPUTERS

by Gojko Adzic

CONTENTS

INTRODUCTION

There's no doubt that computers are running our world, having the final say on everything from the price of your morning cup of coffee to global foreign exchange rates. Governments around the world are quickly becoming digital. Jobs are getting replaced with algorithms. Ubiquitous automation, along with some clever marketing, tricks us into believing that phones, TV sets and even cars are somehow smart. Yet all those computer systems were created by people – people who are well-meaning but fallible and biased, clever but forgetful, and who have grand plans but are pressed for time. Digitising a piece of work doesn't mean there will be no mistakes, but instead guarantees that when mistakes happen, they'll run at a massive scale.

This book is about people caught between bad assumptions and binary logic. You'll read about humans who are invisible to computers, how a default password caused a zombie apocalypse and why airlines sometimes give away free tickets. This is also a book on how to prevent, avoid and reduce the impact of such silly problems.

FOR THE IMPATIENT

The Inverse Monkey Rule part, starting from page 183, contains checklists and heuristics that you can use during development, analysis and testing.

As a professional software developer, I'm much more guilty than the average person of driving civilisation towards a digital apocalypse. At the same time, I've been on the wrong end of a computer bug frequently enough to appreciate the pain that such a thing can create. This book is my attempt to raise awareness about some common and dangerous, but perfectly preventable, types of software blunders. I also want to help ordinary people fight back against digital monsters.

Knowing what kind of mistakes software developers are likely to make helped me open a bank account against the better judgement of a robotic workflow, resolve extortionate utility bills and recover my debit card after it was kidnapped by an angry ATM. The next time you bang your head against a software wall, the stories in this book will help you understand better what's going on and show you where to look for problems. If nothing else, when it seems as if you're under a black-magic spell, these stories will at least allow you to see the lighter side of the binary chaos.

For my colleagues involved in software delivery, I hope this book helps you find more empathy for people suffering from our mistakes, as it's always people who pay the price in the end. My intention with this book is to illustrate some typical, common mistakes with memorable stories, not to create a comprehensive guide for software quality. However, the final part of the book contains some nice tips and tricks, combined from all the stories, that you can use to make your software less error prone.

ARTIFICIAL BUT NOT INTELLIGENCE

Our lives are increasingly tracked, monitored and categorised by software, driving a flood of information into the vast sea of big data. In this brave new world, humans can't cope with information overload. Governments and companies alike rely on computers to automatically detect fraud, predict behaviour and enforce laws. Inflexible automatons, barely smarter than a fridge, now make life-changing decisions.

But the tax codes, laws and regulations of our world weren't designed with automation in mind. They are ambiguous and context dependent, full of loopholes, exceptions and special cases. The entire legal profession thrives exactly because laws are not binary, and lawyers aren't giving up their lunch to robots any time soon. And, of course, software developers rarely have the expertise to interpret even those regulations that are well defined.

The stories in this part show what happens when inflexible decision-making algorithms run into the diversity of real life.

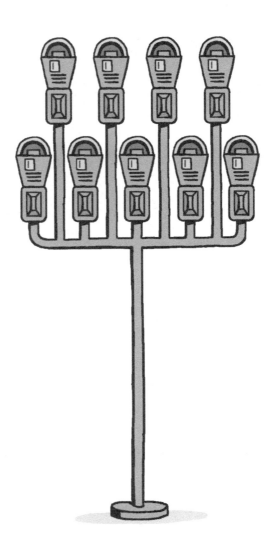

LICENCE
To VOID

Surveillance cameras and machine-readable licence plates make it easier to monitor traffic, charge road tolls and issue fines. But when computers can't process licence plates, the system becomes easy to exploit. Even though Silicon Valley is at the forefront of technology, the state of California, USA, lost more than $12 million in 2013 alone in uncollected toll revenue, because computers couldn't charge drivers of cars without licence plates. Although in most of the world cars require licence plates, the California Vehicle Code 4456, section C2, allows a new car to be driven without licence plates for up to 90 days. One of the most famous abusers of that loophole was Steve Jobs, who reportedly leased a brand new silver Mercedes-Benz SL55 AMG every few months, just so he could drive anonymously. California bill AB-516 is planned to end the exploit in 2019, but there will still be cars with licence plates that are difficult to recognise or even missing. And when traffic officers try to issue tickets to cars without licence plates, computers go crazy.

The most famous case in point is that of Robert Barbour from Los Angeles. Barbour was fond of sailing and wanted to get custom licence plates. His top two choices were BOATING and SAILING. Barbour didn't want anything else, but the form had three fields and they were all mandatory. So in the third choice field, he wrote 'no plate'. In a prophetic mistake that would keep happening throughout the next few months, a computer at the Department of Motor Vehicles interpreted literally something that humans would easily understand as a missing piece of data. Barbour's first two choices were already taken, so the licence plate was issued for his third choice. Having a licence that said 'no plate' sounded quirky enough, so Barbour decided not to complain. But the fun stopped a month later, when he started receiving notices for parking fines from all over California. When an illegally parked vehicle did not have a licence plate, the officers still had to issue a ticket, but computers just wouldn't take no for an answer. Officers had to find a workaround and, humans being humans, many had the same idea as Barbour. The officers just issued the fine for 'no plate'. Those tickets would normally not end up anywhere, but all of a sudden computers had something to match them against. By the time Barbour's trouble caught the attention of the media, he was getting more than 2000 parking tickets per month.

When the California Department of Motor Vehicles finally caught up with what was going on, it advised its officers to stop using 'no plate' as the marker for missing plates. Instead of fixing the computer systems to accept tickets without licence plates, the department came up with a different workaround. Officers were officially supposed to use the marker 'missing'. This immediately started causing a lot of trouble for Andrew Burg in Marina del Rey. Burg, imagine the coincidence, already owned the licence plate MISSING. A similar thing happened to Carol Schroeder from Florida, who got a custom NOTAG plate and shortly after received demands for about $8000 of unpaid tickets. Ralph August, from Westchester, had a similar experience with his licence plate UNKNOWN. Scottie Roberson from Huntsville, Alabama, chose a vanity licence plate that combined his lucky number, 7, and his nickname, Racer X. Unfortunately, XXXXXXX was popular among traffic officers in the city of Birmingham, just a hundred miles away, as a marker for missing plates. Roberson ended up receiving more than $19,000 of parking tickets before the media put pressure on local officials to deal with the problem.

The absolute winner in this category is Richard Turner of Beverly Hills, who had the licence plate VOID. A few years after he got the vanity plates, the local Department of Motor Vehicles changed the way it handled tickets dismissed by courts, and started marking them as void. Of course, computers couldn't be upgraded so quickly, so people just typed VOID into the licence plate field, and Turner started receiving all the tickets.

Such mistakes happen when a computer insists that humans provide a piece of information that isn't immediately available or just doesn't exist, so people find workarounds. The real fun starts when several systems need to exchange information, and they all use different workarounds. The placeholders in one part become valid data for another, and errors multiply and propagate.

Problems with data markers can stay dormant for a long time. Once all the records that were never expected to match anything start to relate to a valid piece of information, such as someone finally getting the 'no plate' plates, chaos starts.

On the opposite side of the problem, algorithms ignoring the information they should have matched from other systems cause even bigger problems, as the next story shows.

GET OUT OF JAIL FREE

A car flew down Penrose Street in Sun Valley, California, USA, on 10 July 2010. Behind the wheel was Javier Joseph Rueda, then 28 years old, who had recently been released from prison. Rueda was one of 10,000 people on non-revocable parole (NRP) who were let out early because a computer thought they were so low risk and so unlikely to repeat crimes that they didn't even have to report to a parole officer. Earlier that day, a policeman had tried to stop Rueda, suspecting that he was driving while intoxicated. If an NRP was caught committing a crime, he would have to go back behind bars. So, Javier decided to risk it all and try to outrun the patrol car. But the flashing lights and the siren tailing Rueda were not giving up. By the time the chase reached Penrose Street, Rueda was reconsidering his options. He stopped the car and got out, turned to the police patrol, and pulled out two semi-automatic handguns.

California had a huge problem with prison overcrowding even before the subprime mortgage bubble exploded in 2007. The subsequent global financial crisis only made things worse. The state had the capacity to incarcerate around 80,000 people, but the prison population in 2009 was almost double that. A special federal court ordered California to reduce overcrowding by 30,000 over two years, because some prisoners couldn't get even the minimum medical care. The US Supreme Court later confirmed the decision, arguing that the conditions were so bad they violated the constitutional ban on cruel punishment. State officials were left with an almost unsolvable problem of dealing with significantly more people on parole without additional supervisors or funding.

The way out of the crisis was NRPs, introduced in 2010. People given NRP were low-risk offenders who were not gang members and did not have a history of violence. NRPs were released into unsupervised parole, leaving the officers to deal with high risk individuals. To quickly select thousands of people who fitted the profile for early release, the state turned to an experimental software system called the Parole Violation Decision-Making Instrument (PVDMI). PVDMI found some 10,000 people, who got an early taste of freedom. Javier Rueda was one of them.

After serving just two years of a ten-year sentence, Rueda was classified by PVDMI as someone who wasn't likely to commit crime again, at least not a violent one. This was despite the fact that he was a known gang member with a history of assault on police officers, and that his crime included a firearms violation. The police patrol tailing Rueda to Penrose Street soon found out exactly how low risk and non-violent he was. One of the patrol men got shot, but the other returned fire. In the end, Javier managed to avoid going back to prison, but perhaps at a higher price than he was expecting to pay.

As usual, journalists did better work than computers. Two months before the incident, the San Diego Union Tribune warned about the early-release programme. The Tribune claimed that roughly 650 NRPs fitted a high risk category, including gang members and violent rapists. Rueda's shooting caused a manual review of several hundred cases, leading the state's Office of the Inspector General to admit mistakes. According to the revised estimate, more than 450 released prisoners posed a high risk of violence, and more than 1000 had a high risk of committing drug crimes.

PVDMI did not have access to the arrest history for many inmates, and, because of software bugs, people with incomplete profiles were classified as low risk. The review concluded that the error rate was an alarming 15%.

The Washington State Department of Corrections repeated the mistake, releasing more than 3000 people too early. This glitch was caused by an overly enthusiastic computer system that shortened sentences based on good behaviour. Some categories of crimes prevented an early release, but a software bug assigned good behaviour credits even to ineligible prisoners. As a result, roughly 3% of the inmates released over a decade got out too early. The bug was identified in 2012 when the family of a crime victim complained to the DOC about the early release of the offender. Investigators manually calculated the perpetrator's release date and spotted the mistake, but it took the DOC more than three years to fix the problem. By that time, more than 100 of those released early had been arrested again for committing crimes while on parole. After the media put pressure on politicians, Dan Pacholke, Secretary of the DOC, lost his job over the blunder. Unfortunately, other people paid a much higher price for those mistakes. Ceasar Medina, then 17 years old, and Lindsay Hill, a 35-year-old mother of two, were killed by former inmates who should have still been behind bars according to their original sentences.

People designing these systems made, in retrospect, silly mistakes. But the consequences were far from trivial. One system considered the lack of history as confirmation that there was nothing suspicious, and the other decided there was nothing suspicious despite the history available to it.

Sometimes, too much history causes problems as well. When Steven Lawrence Wright walked out of the downtown Inmate Reception Center in Los Angeles on 30 January 2016, he could hardly believe his luck. Wright had been convicted for an attempted murder and was in prison awaiting sentencing. Meanwhile, he was called to testify in a different murder case as a witness, and flatly refused. The judge punished him with a five-day sentence for contempt of court. When those five days were over, due to a mix of clerical errors and computer case-management problems, Wright got his release papers and the guards walked him out of the door. Wright was probably confused, but didn't complain. A week-long manhunt across the USA followed, and the FBI managed to capture Wright again in Boulder City, Nevada.

It seems that multiple concurrent sentences, especially if imposed by different authorities, cause mysterious problems for computers. Ilija B was a member of the notorious Pink Panthers gang, which organised more than 300 jewellery robberies in 35 countries, stealing an estimated €330 million. He was originally arrested in Germany and sentenced to six years. After Ilija had served half of the sentence, the Austrian authorities wanted him for a murder trial, so he was transferred. Ilija was then sentenced to an six additional years, but the computers miscalculated his release date and failed to include the remaining part of the German sentence. As a result, Ilija walked out three years too soon in 2014. With Ilija being such a high profile case, the authorities quickly recognised the mistake, but he was already gone.

These kinds of issues arise in case-management systems because small testing samples rarely reflect the diversity of the real world, especially over a long period of time. When most people in a category have a single item, such as a single sentencing record, it's easy to make an unthinking assumption that one and only one such record will exist in all cases. That's how multiple concurrent sentences end up being treated incorrectly, and how the lack of sentencing records caused computers to be too trusting.

On a more positive note, computer errors aren't always on the side of crime. In 2008, prison computers in Sudbury Prison, in the UK, raised an alarm that Michael John Glover had escaped. After a failed manhunt, guards discovered Glover in his cell, where he'd been all the time. The prison was forced to publicly apologise for a false alarm.

Bad assumptions about what's possible or not possible are even more tricky if users can enter the related information themselves, as the next story shows nicely.

-1 BOOKS

Amazon, the online 'everything store', is famous for business experiments and relentless customer focus. Jeff Bezos, the key man behind Amazon's huge success, explained the core strategy in an interview with the Washington Post in 2013. 'We've had three big ideas at Amazon that we've stuck with for 18 years, and they're the reason we're successful. Put the customer first. Invent. And be patient.' Inventing led to lots of experiments that got killed, most famously the Kindle Fire phone. Customers didn't seem to find that particularly interesting, no matter how patient Amazon was. On the other hand, quick experimentation led to a ton of fantastic discoveries, such as the behaviour-based search, which brought the company millions of dollars. Yet, even with its focus on customers being the first item in the immortal strategy, Amazon still decided to kill one particular feature that customers found incredibly useful. Being able to order –1 books.

In an interview with Richard Brandt, the author of the book One Click, Bezos said, 'We found that customers could order a negative quantity of books! And we would credit their credit card with the price and, I assume, wait around for them to ship the books.' In the book Amazon Hacks, the discovery of this feature is credited to Jonathan Leblang, one of the early Amazon customers who joined the online store as a developer in 1999 and still works there.

This was obviously a great customer-centric feature. It's also a fantastic example of how software quality is not something that can be measured on a simple scale. For Amazon, this was obviously bad. But for users, negative quantity actually brought positive quality.

Of course, trusting users to enter anything is always going to lead to problems. When I started working professionally as a developer, during the dotcom boom, one of my first assignments was to figure out how some users were able to obtain huge discounts in an online store. With a bit of logging, a colleague and I discovered that the shopping cart was submitting prices from the web browser, and the back-end blindly trusted it. People with a bit of HTML knowledge could just edit the page and set their own price for anything.

Although every few months someone uploads a new video to YouTube showing how to apply a similar trick to smaller web stores (search for 'tamper data shopping'), as an industry we've generally learned to validate user inputs. Still, the negative quantity problem keeps happening.

For example, the Red Hat Cloud Installer was affected by such a bug in 2016, where entering a negative quantity for the number of subscriptions activated all possible subscriptions. And it's not just shopping carts that suffer from this problem. The popular virtualisation container management software Kubernetes allowed users to request a negative amount of memory or CPU power, which would then cause other containers to be placed into hosts where they couldn't fit.

The reason why these problems keep happening is people might think they're managing conceptual values such as quantity, but computers only care about numbers. Some conceptual values might not make sense in real life, such as negative quantity, so they are easy to overlook. Computers will happily translate them into numbers, though.

With order management systems the problem is even trickier, because negative quantity sometimes actually makes sense. For example, negative inventory might be a consequence of selling too much. This is far from a software bug – it might actually mean that the business is doing better than expected. It's often much better to allow the inventory to go slightly negative and order more supplies than to reject a sale.

When the same concept makes sense for one part of a large system but is meaningless in another, edge cases often lead to bad assumptions and software problems. Customer service staff might try putting in negative orders to signal returns from customers. That leads to some intriguing conversations between developers and users on whether something is an issue or a feature, such as the comment 'This is not a bug, because it's a negative receipt not a return' on the IBM Maximo Asset Management support site.

Negative quantities are a great way to play parts of a system against each other, because people often make different assumptions about them, especially if there is a workflow in which steps can be reversed. For example, the Intuit Quick Books Point of Sale software had a bug that would break purchase orders because one part of the process supported negative quantities, but another part just ignored them. Users were able to enter items received against a purchase order, then reverse it (for example, to undo a bad entry), then book the items again, and the purchase order would end up in a broken state. Reversals would try to remove items by submitting a negative quantity, but the entry system didn't allow negative quantities, so that part just got ignored.

Trusting users to enter correct information led to so many problems in the early days of Internet that most software developers today actually do a good job validating inputs, and preventing silly problems. However, as an industry we still have to learn the lesson of similarly distrusting computers, as the next few stories show.

PEPSI 349

On the morning of 17 December 2015, John Brookings, Jr, and Richard Spense became millionaires, at least on paper. Brookings bought a winning Keno ticket from a shop in New Castle County in Delaware, USA. Five minutes later, Spense walked into the same shop, bought a ticket, and also won. Each prize was worth $1 million. Keno is a number-guessing instant lottery game, with drawings in Delaware every four minutes. Having two winners in the same location within such a short period is highly unlikely. In fact, it was so unlikely that the Delaware Lottery refused to pay up.

After an investigation lasting several months, Delaware Lottery director, Vernon Kirk, released a statement blaming a software glitch. The random-number generator used for Keno had stopped issuing new numbers for 20 minutes, and the lottery's 'automated draw machine' had apparently decided that the best course of action was to just reuse old numbers. As a result, according to Kirk, the five draws during the glitch were predictable. Apologising for any inconvenience, the lottery offered to refund the tickets for the five games, but wasn't going to pay any prizes.

Sure, drawing the same set of numbers in sequence is highly unlikely, but not any more unlikely than drawing any two particular sets of numbers. In this age of computers, games of chance seem to have changed meaning. They are no longer about hoping for a highly unlikely event, but instead about fitting within some particular set of business expectations, known only to the people who set up the game. And if the house doesn't like the outcome, even if the mathematical probabilities haven't changed, it's easy to blame computers. At the same time, computers do whatever they're told, even if that's as stupid as reusing old numbers.

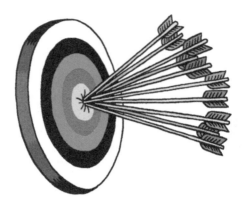

Brookings and Spense sued the lottery in November 2016, asking for their $2 million. At the time when I wrote this in 2017, the case was still going through the courts. The interesting question for the legal experts will be whether the two men signed up for the game that the lottery hoped was implemented, or the game that was actually implemented. The case is not at all clear cut, and there are arguments for both sides. For example, in a typically Canadian act, the British Columbia Lottery Corporation decided to retroactively distribute CAD$1 million of winnings after it discovered a bug in 2015, and to reimburse players who lost money during the glitch.

With the easy excuse of saying computers have got it wrong, winning the lottery doesn't necessarily mean you've actually won the lottery these days. Going back even before Brookings and Spense, on 19 October 2008, Virginia Lottery refused to pay out winnings for the Fast Play Super 7 game. With a $2 ticket and some basic arithmetic skills, players could try their luck at winning $7,777 by adding up numbers on a pre-printed grid. By 9am, the lottery had received enough calls from retailers, panicking because of too many winning tickets, to shut the game down. Out of the total 2336 tickets sold in the period, more than 600 were 'printed incorrectly' according to the Virginia Lottery spokesman John Hagerty.

Sometimes people win, but not as much as they expected. For example, the Illinois Lottery quick-pick machines started to reprint old numbers after a software upgrade in May 2012, leading to 340 duplicate prize-winners. Other times, the wrong numbers are announced because of some other software messing things up. The Louisiana Lottery announced winning numbers for its Pick 3 and Pick 4 games on 12 March 2017 as 1-1-1 and 2-2-2-2, then quickly retracted it, blaming 'some kind of technical problem' at the Louisiana Public Broadcasting corporation. Similarly, the Washington Lottery published the wrong numbers for its Veterans Raffle in January 2013.

Computers are great for repeatable and reliable automation, the exact opposite of randomness. And although it's possible to simulate chance events with specialist hardware, choosing a random number is a very small piece of the whole system for playing games and delivering results. Small software glitches in other parts of the system can throw things off significantly and change the probabilities, effectively rigging the game.

The US State Department had to void the draw for its diversity visa in May 2011, due to a software glitch, even after it had published the official results. The diversity visa, popularly known as the green card lottery, started in 1994 as a way to bring immigrants from under-represented communities to the USA. In 2011, more than 19 million people applied, and 90,000 were randomly selected to proceed to the next step. However, the department discovered that over 90% of the winners were among the people who'd signed up in the first two days of the application period, raising doubts about whether this was a fair choice as required by US law.

Although it's easy to dismiss all these problems as small software bugs, it's imperative to also understand the potential effects on the people on the other side of those glitches, especially for life-changing events such as winning the state lottery or being allowed to immigrate. Changing the results after they're published is guaranteed to make people feel cheated, and blaming the situation on computers isn't much of an excuse. Pepsi learned that lesson way back in 1992...

In a major marketing drive in the Philippines, Pepsi invited people, through ads on TV and radio and in major newspapers, to buy its soft drink and have a chance of becoming a millionaire. Each bottle cap had a number, and one of the lucky owners was destined to get a million pesos, tax free (about US$40,000 back then). Sales soared. On 25 May 1992, in an eagerly anticipated TV event, Pepsi published the winning number: 349. The only problem was that instead of a single winning bottle cap, more than 800,000 bottle caps marked 349 were in circulation.

Pepsi blamed a software glitch and refused to pay, but significantly underestimated the backlash. In a mini revolution, mobs stoned and torched delivery trucks. Protesters threw Molotov cocktails at Pepsi plants and offices. Local Pepsi executives hastily decided to offer 500 pesos (about US$20) to anyone who brought in a winning cap before 12 June 1992. Expecting only a few thousand claimants, the company was in panic mode when 490,116 bottle caps turned up. Instead of the US$2 million budgeted for winnings, Pepsi paid out almost US$10 million in a 'goodwill' gesture, but that wasn't enough to stop the tide. Protests continued well into the next year. On 13 February 1993, someone even threw a grenade at a parked Pepsi truck in Manila. The explosive device bounced off and killed a five-year-old girl and injured six people. More than 22,000 people took the matter to court, in roughly 700 civil suits and more than 5200 criminal complaints for fraud and deception. The blunder was only finally put to bed in 2006, after a ruling from the Supreme Court of the Philippines.

A common thread in all these stories is that the random results were too random and surprised the organisers. And although it might be perfectly fine to cancel and void a game of chance due to a technical glitch, timing really is everything. I doubt anyone would have cried foul if the US State Department had discovered the wrong distribution of diversity visas before the results were published, and just postponed the lottery. And if Pepsi executives had voided the draw and re-scheduled it for a few days later in 1992, some people might have been annoyed, but it's unlikely that anyone would have thrown hand grenades at Pepsi trucks.

The key lesson here is that information provided by computers should not be blindly trusted, especially if it needs to fit into some kind of strict business context such as equal representation or total prize pay-out value. Problems caused by blindly trusting computers get even worse when a bunch of different software systems get involved. To illustrate just how problematic this can get, we need to take a trip to Kansas.

THE HAUNTED FARM IN THE MIDDLE OF AMERICA

Ashburn is a little town in Virginia, USA, home to just over 50,000 people. More than 90% of its adult residents work in white-collar jobs. The town is well above the US average in terms of education and income, and crime rates are significantly lower than in the rest of the country. By all counts, Ashburn is a safe, quiet, middle-class residential area for people working in Washington DC, just 40 minutes away by car. But one house, smack in the middle of town, was apparently a hotbed of international crime. Rather than being about the real-life inspiration for Breaking Bad, however, this story sprang from two foolish assumptions cemented into bad software.

At the centre of the fictitious international crime ring was Anthony Pav, who lived at the end of a cul-de-sac near Ashburn Lake. The problems started suddenly in 2012. Pav returned home one night to find police vans outside his house. The officers were looking for a stolen government laptop, which had apparently phoned back from Pav's address. Investigators tore the house up, found nothing, and left Pav confused. Soon Pav started getting calls from people searching for stolen mobile phones and messages on Facebook from random people accusing him of online abuse. He was the only person in the neighbourhood affected by mysterious accusations of crime, as if his home were cursed by some kind of modern black magic. It took almost four years and some excellent investigative journalism to finally pinpoint what was haunting Pav's house.

When stolen laptops and phones call back home, they send information about a current Internet Protocol (IP) address – effectively a location pointer in the digital world. But that's not enough to dispatch a police car, so law enforcement agencies use software systems to translate addresses between the digital and the physical world. Pav's curse was not caused by witchcraft, but by over 17 million IP addresses pointing to his house.

The first part of the problem was that IP addresses were never intended to reliably point to a physical location, or even to stay in the same physical place. Internet addresses were intended to help computers talk to each other through various intermediaries, dynamically discovering the best route to send digital packets. In the days before home broadband Internet, individuals would get a temporary IP address for each connection, and there wasn't much point even trying to translate these into physical addresses. My first Internet provider charged significantly more if you wanted the same address every time you connected, as that was seen as a premium business feature, not something individuals cared about.

With broadband Internet connections, physical addresses started getting a more permanent IP number as well. At the same time, web applications became more dynamic. It became useful for services to know the rough geographic location of their users, so they could automatically adjust the language or geographic preferences. Because there's no official directory translating digital addresses into physical ones, independent geolocation services emerged to collect this information informally. The most popular one is MaxMind, which can provide the approximate latitude and longitude associated with a digital pointer. By connecting MaxMind information to a postal database, it became possible to discover the home addresses of some Internet users.

As Internet crime picked up, the physical location of an IP address became the first clue for both law enforcement and amateur investigators. For example, in 2011 the authorities arrested a bus driver in Poolesville, Maryland, USA, for downloading child pornography.

The key piece of information leading the investigators back to the driver was his home IP address.

IP addresses might be a good first clue, but they are hardly incriminating evidence. It's trivially easy to spoof an address by using a virtual private network service, which would make it look as if the user were located in a huge data centre.

The second part of the problem was that software developers translating MaxMind data into postal addresses trusted the data too much. According to Thomas Mather, the founder of MaxMind, the database was never intended to point to a single house, but to a rough geographic area. And the database was never sold as 100% correct. In some instances, MaxMind only knew the city where the IP address was located. In cases such as that one, it would point to the latitude and longitude of the geographic centre of the city.

With a perfect mix of imprecise information and using IP addresses for an unintended purpose, and due to the fact that the results were correct most of the time, nobody noticed the outliers – for example, that all the addresses allocated to two massive data centres owned by Google and Facebook in Ashburn pointed somewhere close to Pav's house. As cloud computing took off, Google started renting out spare capacity to other service providers. Any time any users of those third-party services did something wrong, amateur investigators would quickly jump to conclusions without really understanding how the Internet works. And Pav would get all the blame.

Anthony Pav was not the only one whose home was haunted by digital crime ghosts. In Atlanta, Georgia, USA, Christina Lee and Michael Saba got frequent visits from people looking for lost mobile phones. The police came by several times and even detained them while looking for a missing person.

But the worst case was a farm in northern Kansas, close to the border with Nebraska, occupied by James and Theresa Arnold. A few days after the Arnolds moved in, the police came looking for a stolen truck. Over the next few years, various government agents investigated the Arnolds for tax fraud, missing people, bitcoin scams, stolen credit cards, identity theft and almost any other digital crime you can think of. The local sheriff received weekly reports about scams originating from the farm. Ambulances came looking for suicidal patients. Angry people phoned the Arnolds to complain about Internet service problems, such as not being able to send e-mail. Internet vigilantes published the Arnolds' personal information online, as revenge for some unknown offence. Someone left a broken toilet seat in the driveway.

The story was finally unravelled in 2016 by Kashmir Hill, a journalist writing for Fusion, who discovered that over 600 million IP addresses pointed to the Arnolds' Kansas farm. If MaxMind only knew that an IP address was in the USA, but not where, it would point to the geographic centre. And, as you can probably guess, the closest house was the Arnolds'.

Until Hill's investigation, the people at MaxMind weren't even aware how much trouble their default locations for imprecise mapping were causing. To their defence, the problem was caused by other people taking MaxMind information too literally and using it for a completely unintended purpose. After the story broke, Max-Mind quickly relocated imprecise addresses to the middles of lakes or to other places far from people. However, the Arnolds decided to sue the company for years of harassment. At the time when I wrote this, in June 2017, the case was still going through the courts.

Problems such as these happen because many consumer applications today get built on top of a whole pyramid of cloud computing services, coupled with a mistaken belief that external computers are always right. Most applications won't blindly trust the data supplied by users, but for some reason data supplied by computers gets accepted without questioning. Even worse, as information from different sources gets mashed up together, the margin of error becomes much higher, but validating the source information becomes a lot more difficult. Most people disturbing the Arnolds thought they were doing the right thing, but they were making bad decisions based on wrong data. Of course, to make this problem even worse, we need to take the humans out of the equation, and let computers make decisions based on bad data provided by other computers.

THE OLDER YOUNGER BROTHER

In the early hours of 14 January 2015, thousands of people arrived for work in Brisbane, Australia, only to find their offices still closed. Busy parents tried to drop children off to school, but faced shut gates. People wandered around the central business district desperately looking for coffee, but the shops were still closed. It was as if a significant portion of the population had suddenly lost track of time. A few hours later, the local radio stations found a culprit. Claire Wong, a spokesperson for Optus, a major mobile phone provider in the area, was busy apologising for waking people up too early.

Some Australian states use daylight saving time between October and April, but not Queensland. The Optus mobile phone towers in south-east Queensland somehow felt this was unfair and decided to move the clock forward by one hour and give the residents a bit more chance to enjoy the sun. Computers today tend to trust other computers blindly, so most mobile phones connected to Optus automatically obeyed and adjusted their internal clocks. People who used a mobile phone alarm to wake up, and naturally trusted the time on the phone, ended up jamming the roads around Brisbane a full hour too early. The glitch also affected customers of some other networks that used the Optus infrastructure, such as Virgin. Social media, of course, lit up with curses and complaints. People with wrist watches finally got a chance to prove that dumb clocks still have a use. Trying to put a nicer spin on the whole story, Optus promised via its Facebook page to give a free coffee to all the affected users in Brisbane.

Daylight saving time is a great example of a regular irregularity. It repeats every year, at a predictable interval, but it breaks how people normally observe time. This almost guarantees that someone will do something stupid on the days after switching to daylight saving time. Tameside council in Greater Manchester, UK, got into trouble in October 2016 when its staff moved the clock on the Hyde Town Hall one hour forward instead of back, creating a two-hour difference between the official time and the time shown on the clock on the tower.

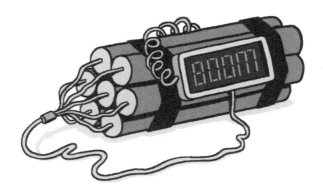

Luckily, most people today have more than one way of tracking time. But that can also cause problems if different clocks need to be synchronised. In the early morning hours of 2 April 2014, an explosive device planted under a Volvo in Dublin, Ireland, went off, and witnesses saw a severely injured man fleeing the scene. Police suspected that the bomb had exploded too early, while the suspect was trying to plant it, because he'd forgotten to switch the bomb timer forward after the change to daylight saving time.

With ubiquitous mobile phones, we've become accustomed to someone else handling the whole problem of setting the correct time. The Internet made it easy to magically update millions of clocks, but the flip-side is that small glitches can cause huge impacts. The solution, of course, is not to trust external time updates blindly. But that just shifts the responsibility for tracking time zones to individual gadgets, which are also not perfect.

A case in point is the town of Dunedin, on the southern tip of New Zealand. On 4 April 2010, clocks went back an hour in New Zealand as daylight saving time ended. Around 80 parking meters in Dunedin decided to rebel against central control and switched back to daylight saving time at midnight the next day. For many car drivers, the result was a buy one, get one free discount on parking, because the permits expired a whole hour later than they should have. The glitch happened during the Easter holidays, when the software support people were on a break, so the council staff had to manually reset the clocks the next morning. And, of course, the next midnight, the defiant parking meters turned on daylight saving again. The dance continued for several days.

Six years later, Dunedin parking meters were in the news again. This time, they'd miscounted the time in the other direction. When daylight saving time began in September 2016, 16 out of 350 parking meters in the city refused to accept it. Motorists paying for one hour of parking got tickets that immediately expired, but council staff weren't aware of the glitch and kept issuing fines.

Keeping track of time zone changes is an especially big problem for autonomous devices, supposed to work without a lot of human contact. With nobody to complain quickly, small problems can stay undiscovered for an extended period and cost quite a lot of money. Continuing the great tradition of rebellious traffic equipment in New Zealand, a speed camera in Ngauranga Gorge, close to Wellington, went rogue on 5 May 2015. After daylight saving time ended, it correctly switched back to the regular time zone, but then decided to go back to daylight saving after all. Over the next three days, the camera issued automatic speeding tickets with incorrect time-stamps. When the glitch was discovered, some 1700 offenders won the daylight saving lottery, because the police had to cancel more than NZ$151,000 in fines.

Time zone changes can also cause difficulties for planning future events. For example, it might seem that scheduling something for the same time tomorrow is as easy as adding 24 hours. That approach actually works well in most cases. However, the definition of 'same time' becomes a bit trickier when the politics of daylight saving come into the play. The same time tomorrow, according to official government clocks, might be one hour earlier or later than the same time according to the Earth's rotation. iPhone 4 owners learned that lesson the hard way when central Europe switched back one hour on 1 November 2010. The phones updated their clocks but forgot to re-schedule the alarms. As a result, social media was full of people who'd woken up one hour too late, complaining about over-sleeping and being late for work.

A particular cause of problems with daylight saving time is the assumption that time zone differences don't change. As with any other rule invented by people, daylight saving is subject to politics. When bored politicians decide to wake their subjects up early, computers also need to be updated. Israel decided to synchronise time zone changes with Europe in 2013, moving the end of summer time from early September to late October. But the message somehow didn't get through to those responsible for software calendars. Mobile phones manufactured by pretty much all the major players decided to switch to winter time a full seven weeks before schedule. The problem also affected popular online calendar and e-mail applications.

Daylight saving requires serious consideration for any software system that deals with time, because it's a great cause of confusion for people and machines alike, and sometimes leads to quirky situations that break normal rules of logic. The best example of that is Ronan Peterson, born on 6 November 2013 at the Cape Cod Hospital in Massachusetts, USA. He was both older and younger than his twin brother, Samuel, born some 30 minutes before – or after, depending on who you ask. Samuel came out first, at 1:39am. As Emily Peterson was busy trying to give birth to the second twin, Massachusetts moved the clock back one hour, so Ronan officially joined his brother at 1:10am, causing a good deal of confusion among hospital staff.

Although Samuel and Ronan didn't break any computers when they were born, twins can cause quite a lot of confusion for digital intelligence as well, especially when blind trust in computers meets blind trust in biometric information. That's the subject of the next story.

THE KENNEDY SISTERS FRAUD

Alicia and Alicen Kennedy walked into the local Department of Motor Vehicles (DMV) office in Evans, Georgia, USA, in October 2015. Excited at the prospect of finally getting drivers' licences, the sisters handed in their paperwork, but the DMV clerk wouldn't let them take the test. The computer refused Alicia's photo. She took another picture, then another one, and the computer just kept refusing them. The pair had to sign the application forms over and over. The clerk finally gave up and called the headquarters. Alicen overheard the phone conversation between the clerk and the IT wizards in the central tower. Apparently, one of the sisters had got caught by a fraud detection net, and nobody could understand why.

After an investigation, the Georgia Department of Driver Services concluded that the computers couldn't tell the twins apart and insisted that they were the same person. This led the robot overlords to conclude that someone was trying to scam the system by taking the test under two different names, so they kept blocking both applications.

Biometric checks sound incredibly promising for reducing fraud and mistakes caused by human perception, but they are not foolproof, regardless of how magical they might sound to a layman. For example, HSBC bank in the UK allowed customers to verify their identity with just voice recognition, capturing more than 100 unique personal characteristics with a single sentence. But the bank fell into the same trap as the Georgia DMV. Dan Simmons, a journalist working for the BBC, managed to fool the voice authentication with his twin brother.

Twins often do look alike, so the story of the Kennedy sisters is almost understandable. But for John Gass from Natick, Massachusetts, USA, a similar photo recognition problem ended up being a lot more serious. On 5 April 2011, he received a letter from the Massachusetts Registry of Motor Vehicles saying that his driver's licence had been revoked, effective from five days earlier. Gass had not committed any traffic violations or received any other penalties for several years, so suddenly losing his licence came as a shock. He immediately phoned the registry, but staff refused to explain why the licence had been revoked, and only suggested that Gass could reinstate it if he could prove his identity. After ten days of phone calls and a legal hearing at the registry, the mystery was finally solved. An automated photo recognition system for an antiterrorism database had flagged Gass, because the computers thought he matched a photo of a known criminal. To human eyes, however, it was easy to see that Gass and the criminal were two completely different people. In some ways, it's lucky that Gass only wasted ten days due to this error. A mistaken match in an antiterrorism database could have had significantly more serious consequences.

Computer image detection has improved dramatically in the last decade, and for some purposes computers are now better than people. For example, in 2017, Google researchers trained an artificial intelligence system to recognise signs of breast cancer in pathology images significantly more accurately and faster than experienced pathologists. Using a known database of images from the Radboud University Medical Center, Google AI achieved a score of 89%. Expert radiologists scored 73%. Still, image recognition is far from perfect. Combined with the trend of 'smart' products, this can cause some quite confusing glitches.

Nikon, the Japanese camera manufacturer, tried to help amateur photographers take better snaps by making their cameras more intelligent. The Nikon Coolpix S630 could recognise when someone in the picture was blinking and warn that the photo was far from ideal. But Joz Wang, a Taiwanese–American consultant, discovered that the camera refused to take pictures of her family, because it falsely detected their eyes as closed. Wang's family come from an East-Asian background, so their eyes just normally appear smaller than those of an average white person. Despite the fact that Nikon is a Japanese company, news agencies around the world poked fun at the 'racist' camera.

The situation is significantly less funny when a government computer makes the same mistake. In December 2016, in New Zealand, Richard Lee's passport application photo was repeatedly rejected by computers, because his eyes were apparently closed. Lee grew up in New Zealand, but his family comes from Taiwan, so he got caught by a similar glitch as Joz Wang.

Of course, people make mistakes all the time when recognising images, so we shouldn't be surprised that computers don't do it perfectly. However, computers tend to incorporate image recognition in a fully automated chain of services, so problems quickly propagate and escalate. In May 2015, Google released a new Photos app that could automatically group images into albums and propose topics. Less than a month later, a photo recognition glitch touched a very difficult nerve in American racial relationships. Jacky Alcine from Brooklyn signed into his photo account and was shocked to see several photos of himself and another African American labelled as gorillas. Although Google responded quickly and removed the erroneous label, and experts pointed out that even some white people got labelled as apes, there was outrage on social media, with people blaming the software for racism.

The problem with many artificial intelligence face recognition systems is that they are only as good as the data sets used for training. Hidden biases of the people who develop such applications can easily find their way into an automated decision process. The US National Institute of Standards and Technology published a comparative study of face recognition algorithms in 2009, concluding that there is a clear 'other-race effect'. Looking at eight algorithms from Western countries and five algorithms from East Asian countries, the study showed how accuracy decreases and false positives increase for faces from a different part of the world.

For minorities that are under-represented in the software development industry, this 'other-race' effect is already a significant issue. In 2009, Wanda Zamen and Desi Cryer, working in the Toppers Camping Center in Waller, Texas, USA, posted a video to YouTube demonstrating the Hewlett Packard MediaSmart camera. MediaSmart has a feature to keep the user in the centre of the frame, making video conferencing easier. When Wanda used the camera, tracking worked perfectly. With Desi in front of the camera and Wanda walking into the frame, the computer decided to follow Wanda immediately and ignore Desi. Even worse, with Desi alone in the frame, the tracking didn't work at all. You can probably guess now that Wanda is white and Desi is an African American. 'Black Desi gets in there, no face recognition any more, buddy', said Cryer, concluding, as a joke, 'HP computers are racist.' The video went viral, got coverage in mainstream media worldwide, and sparked hundreds of articles on racist computers.

Although Zamen and Cryer posted the video as a joke, never expecting to start a racial debate, any kind of light-hearted humour has to stop when you consider the potential effects of similar bugs in government computers. A 2012 study of three face recognition algorithms used by law enforcement companies in the USA concluded that they consistently performed 5–10% worse on photos of African Americans than on those of Caucasians.

People may recognise features of faces similar to theirs better, but computers don't belong to any particular human race, so there's no real need for cross-race effects to spill over to the digital world. Unfortunately, it's quite easy to for people building digital decision makers to unintentionally transfer the hidden biases to their creations.

THE SURPRISING FACTS ABOUT OUR WORLD

Since the dawn of time, we humans have struggled to model the world around us into something more logical. The Earth was supposed to be flat or, when that did not work out, at least perfectly round. The sky was supposed to spin around the Earth, or at least to have the decency to revolve around the Sun. After the French Revolutionary Government declared a decimal calendar, planet Earth flatly refused to change its rotation speed. And, of course, when the Indiana House of Representatives passed bill 246 in 1897, fixing the value of π once and for all to 3.2, no self-respecting circle adjusted its circumference, not even in Indiana. Yes, that would have made squaring a circle significantly easier, but Mother Nature never had any intention of playing according to human rules.

Anyone involved in software delivery faces this same problem every day: we try to shape the world into something more logical, easier to square, or at least simpler to validate. With the elegance of an elephant just noticing a brand new porcelain shop in the neighbourhood, reality often kicks in.

HUBERT BLAINE WOLFE+585,sr

In 1961 IBM introduced a new monster processing system, called 7074. The beast was normally delivered in several trucks, required a room of 40 by 40 feet, and weighed more than 41,000 pounds. The system had a disk storage unit with a capacity of 28 million characters and could process almost 34,000 operations per second. Still, the IBM 7074 was no match for Hubert B. Wolfeschlegelsteinhausenbergerdorff.

Hubert rose to fame in 1964 when Associated Press carried the story of how his name broke the IBM 7074 supercomputer at the John Hancock Mutual Life Insurance Co. Hubert had 26 given names, one for each letter of the alphabet, and 666 letters in his surname. In order to finally get his social security card, Hubert had to clip his name to 44 letters, including spaces, and the application still had to be processed manually instead of on the computer. Hubert decided to use only his eighth given name, the initial letter of his second given name, and the first 35 letters of his surname.

Later in his life, probably as a result of increasing digitisation and the intolerance of computers, Hubert was mostly known as Hubert Blaine Wolfe+585. Hubert passed away in 1997, but that doesn't mean that incredibly long names are a thing of the past. According to the Guinness Book of World Records, the current longest name belongs to Rhoshandiatellyneshiaunneveshenk Koyaanisquatsiuth Williams, a girl born in Texas in 1984, whose actual first name is 1,019 letters long.

Although modern computers work at much more than 34 kHz, unusually long names still break them. In 2013, Janice Keihanaikukauakahihuliheʻekahaunaele started a campaign against the Hawaii Department of Transportation for not being able to print her name on her driving licence. The licences had space for only 34 characters, one fewer than Janice's last name. The driving licences also could not show the ʻokina, the Hawaiian accent that looks like an apostrophe, despite the fact that the native name of Hawaii, Hawaiʻi, also includes the ʻokina.

Journalists from KHON2, a TV station in Honolulu, picked up Janice's story. After public pressure, the government caved in and changed the policy to allow up to 40 characters in a name on a driving licence. This required an upgrade to computer systems across the state.

It's not just long names that cause weird computer problems. Short names do as well. Take, for example, the story of Stephen O, a South Korean living in Virginia, USA. Several of Stephen's credit card applications were rejected because local banking systems could not record a single-letter last name, presumably to prevent people from just entering initials in the registration form. Stephen was only able to get a driving licence under the surname OO. This caused problems when he tried to get car insurance, because the credit agency couldn't match any of the records. The credit agency computers recorded Stephen's last name as Ostephen, presumingly 'upgrading' the name from Korean to Irish. In one database, after a lengthy search, he was found under blank-blank-O. Stephen finally gave up fighting computers and changed his name to Oh.

Although a single-letter last name might sound unusual, it's not that uncommon, especially with romanisation of far-east-Asian names. A notable example is O Rissei, the famous Japanese Go player (Japanese normally write the family name before the given name, so O is his surname). Single-letter given names are also possible. A good example is A Martinez, the American actor famous for his roles in 80s soap operas, who shortened his name from Adolfo to just one letter. Of course, different countries have various rules for name length. For example, Sweden does not allow single-letter names, but the UK does.

With increased computerisation of travel records and identity document systems, bad software causes constant confusion and problems for people with even slightly longer names. Airlines require that the names on a passport exactly match the names on that person's ticket, and government organisations cross-reference passenger data with their own records. But name-length limits vary.

To understand the scale of inconsistency, you just need to check the various standards. For example, the Passenger and Airport Data Interchange Standards of the International Civil Aviation Organization (ICAO) allow up to 64 characters for each of the given name, surname and up to three middle names in passenger records. However, ICAO's guidance on passports requires names to be printed in font size between 10 and 15 characters per inch, which allows up to roughly 40 letters in each of the names. However, the same standard requires the machine-readable part of a passport to fit the full name into 39 letters, including spaces between the words. Some governments impose even shorter limits. For example, Australian passports fit up to 31 characters for name fields, including all spaces.

Even in the same country, systems often have erratic length limits. For example, the US Nonimmigrant Visa Application (DS-160) has space for 31 characters for each name, but the I-94 Arrival/Departure Record fits 17 characters for the last name and only 13 for the given name. The US Social Security Administration accepts two lines of 26 characters per name. The Application for a US Passport (DS-11) allows 21 characters for a last name, 17 for the first given name and 16 for the middle names.

To make things worse, systems not dealing with international travel have their own limits. For example, UK Government Data Standards allow 35 characters for each name, but only 70 characters in total for the full name, consisting of the title, first given name, surname and all middle names. Yet birth certificates are issued for longer names as well. On 31 December 1986, Margaret Nelson from Chesterfield in the UK gave birth to a baby girl. Margaret and her husband, John, wanted to give their newborn daughter 207 names, but that didn't fit on a birth certificate. Eventually the parents settled for just 139 given names. Tracy's full name has 140 words, or 855 letters. When spaces between words are included, the name has 995 characters. Imagine Tracy filling in an immigration form with the field 'any other names you were known by'. For a (slightly) more down-to-earth example of a long name, remember Uma Thurman and Arpad Busson's daughter, Rosalind Arusha Arkadina Altalune Florence Thurman-Busson.

Of course, people can be born with just one given name and then change it to almost anything these days. The UK Deed Poll service allows standard applications with up to 150 characters in a name, but for a special fee accepts even longer names. David Fearn from Walsall, in the West Midlands, changed his name in 2006 to a collection from all the James Bond movies recorded until then. He is now officially known as James Dr No From Russia with Love Goldfinger Thunderball You Only Live Twice On Her Majesty's Secret Service Diamonds Are Forever Live and Let Die The Man with the Golden Gun The Spy Who Loved Me Moonraker For Your Eyes Only Octopussy A View to a Kill The Living Daylights Licence to Kill Golden Eye Tomorrow Never Dies The World Is Not Enough Die Another Day Casino Royale Bond. This James Bond's full name has 69 words or 310 characters without the spaces between words. Just imagine the famous Sean Connery scene at the casino table when he introduces himself as 'Bond, James Bond', but spells out all the other names in between.

Bond movies seem to inspire fanatics. Emma Louise Hodges from Birmingham, in 2012, when she was 28 years old, changed her name to a combination of 14 Bond Girl names. She is now Miss Pussy Galore Honey Rider Solitaire Plenty O'Toole May Day Xenia Onatopp Holly Goodhead Tiffany Case Kissy Suzuki Mary Goodnight Jinx Johnson Octopussy Domino Moneypenny. (Miss is one of her given names, not a title.)

Personal names are critical parts of our identity, so it is important that computers record them correctly. Unfortunately, it's so easy to make wrong assumptions about valid names due to cultural heritage and personal biases. Of course, when it comes to names, length is hardly the only factor confusing computers, as you'll see in the following stories.

GoVeg.com

History books will mostly remember March 2003 for the US invasion of Iraq. The preparations for the war, global protests, UN politics and the first reports of fighting took centre stage in news throughout the month, as if nothing else notable was happening around the world. Trying to grab a moment in the spotlight, a 23-year-old youth educator called Karin Robertson walked into the local city hall in in Norfolk, Virginia, USA, and in a stroke of genius likely broke government computers all over the US.

One of Karin's friends had been through a nasty divorce and legally changed her name to get a clean break from the past. This gave Robertson an idea for how to promote a cause she felt passionate about. Growing up in rural Indiana, the fourth child of a teacher and a biologist, she became interested in how food goes from farm to table. Upon discovering how the meat industry works, Karin become a vegetarian. In the early 2000s, she joined the fight for animal rights at People for the Ethical Treatment of Animals (PETA). The world had just gone through the whole Internet bubble, and while most dot-coms were going bankrupt and disappearing, Karin decided to become one. She updated her records with the city of Norfolk, got a new driving licence and changed her credit cards and utility bills, all under the name GoVeg.com – the domain of a website operated by PETA.

News agencies carried the story of Robertson's crusade all over the world. In accordance with the journalistic practice of balanced reporting, the Chicago Tribune also interviewed Kara Flynn, the spokeswoman for the National Pork Producers Council. Flynn called the name change a 'desperate publicity ploy', but the trick worked and web traffic to GoVeg.com surged.

With punctuation in the middle of her legal name, the activist formerly known as Karin didn't have a first or last name. It was just GoVeg.com, one word. 'I like the whole name together', she said, and got angry when people called her Dot.

Inspired by GoVeg.com's success, other PETA activists followed suit. Christopher Garnett became Kentucky Fried Cruelty.com – this time, the name included spaces. In the UK, Abi Izzard changed her name to StopFortnumAndMasonFoieGras Cruelty.com. Presumably, Cruelty.com was her last name.

Garnett later discovered that the prank prevented him from getting a passport, because various governments systems couldn't match up his records, and changed back to his original name. Even GoVeg.com eventually gave up and reverted to Karin Robertson in 2006.

Just in case you think Internet-inspired names are unique to vegetarians, there is also Terri Iligan from Tennessee, USA. In 2005, the 33-year-old mother of five auctioned the right to change her name, on eBay. Several companies regularly bid on crazy auctions as a way of getting free promotion, including an online casino that won William Shattner's kidney stone. And so, after an auction that netted 15,000 USD, Iligan became GoldenPalace.com. GoldenPalace.com's children apparently started calling her Goldie.

Sure enough, the dot-com naming craze hasn't really taken over the world, but it's dangerous to assume that names can only contain letters and a few other common symbols. For example, in 2004, Jon Cusack from Michigan, USA, gave his son the name Jon Blake Cusack 2.0.

Software systems often need to validate inputs, in order to prevent typos, but judging what exactly is a valid name is a lot more difficult than it might seem at first. In some cases, it requires the courts to get involved. In 1991, a Swedish judge prevented Elisabeth Hallin from naming her son Brfxxccxxmnpcccclllmmnprxvclmnckssqlbb11116 – pronounced Albin. And in Beijing in 2007, when trying to find a unique name for their child among more than 1 billion Chinese people, a couple tried to call their child @ – which the authorities also denied. The New Zealand Registrar of Births, Deaths and Marriages rejected Pat and Sheena Wheaton's attempt to call their son 4Real in 2008. (They called him Superman instead.) However, the same office approved the name Number 16 Bus Shelter.

Wrong assumptions regarding name validation rules can be quite problematic. Someone with unusual symbols in their name might need to register differently in different systems, causing potential problems when all those records need to match. However, acceptable symbols are just a part of the problem. The next story explores another category of name validation rules, that causes even weirder issues.

THEY

In one of the earliest known cases of incorrect user input validation, the cyclops Polyphemus screamed that Nobody was trying to kill him, sending the other cyclopes away instead of calling for help. Taking a trick from Odysseus, a 43-year-old self-employed man called Andrew Wilson, from Branson, Missouri, USA, changed his name to They in 2004. No first name, no last name, just They. I guess They just decided to confuse the world. Apparently the name change was not a way to hide from creditors. In fact, the man formerly known as Wilson is a prolific inventor. Among other things, They patented 'ground-effect lighting', used for a neon-glow effect below cars. They must be very smart.

In most western cultures, it's normal to have a first name and a second name, the latter typically the same for the whole family. Still, it's dangerous to assume that everyone obeys those rules. For a start, people can change their name to almost anything these days, including a single word.

The shorter half of the comedy-magic team Penn & Teller is legally known just as Teller. His driving licence famously reads NFN Teller (NFN is short for no first name). James Hellwig, a professional US wrestler, changed his name to Warrior in a trademark dispute. US software developer Mitch Maddox was officially known as DotComGuy during the dot-com boom, for an online reality show where he was supposed to stay in his house for a year and order all the necessities online.

Well-known cases of people with just one name (fancifully called a mononym) tend to be showbusiness professionals, but don't be fooled into thinking that's a rule. Being born without a last name is infrequent but far from impossible, especially for people from central and south Asia.

Possibly the most famous person with a mononym is Sukarno, the first president of Indonesia. Having a single name was so unusual and difficult for western people to understand that a reporter invented a fictitious first name for Sukarno. The name Achmed Sukarno soon caught on in the media. There are now Wikipedia editing wars for Sukarno's page, in which the first name is continuously added and removed.

The third Secretary-General of the United Nations was Thant, a Burmese national without a last name. In western media, he was commonly known as U Thant, and that name is even on the official UN web page with Thant's profile. However, U was not his first name but the transliteration of a Burmese honorific title, roughly translating to English 'Mr'. For some similar names, check out U Nu (the first Prime Minister of Burma) and U Saw (a Conservative pre-war Prime Minister of British Burma).

Mononymic people often face arbitrary policies, especially when computer systems won't accept no for an answer. Airline booking systems tend to require first and last names separately, and different airlines have different workarounds for single names, such as repeating the name twice or entering a number of Xs in one of the fields. This can create huge problems when several such systems need to match records. Government agencies around the world also tend to have their own workarounds. For example, the UK Identity and Passport Service requires recording the first name with three Xs and using the mononymic name as the surname. The US immigration service often assigns FNU, for first name unknown, as the first name. But there are also cases of people being called LNU (last name unknown), with the mononymic name as the forename.

Those workarounds sometimes start to replace a person's real name, especially if the name is difficult for westerners to pronounce. This was the case with Naqibullah, a former interpreter for the US Armed Forces in Afghanistan, who moved to Houston, USA. When The Wall Street Journal wrote about his case, Naqibullah worked as a taxi driver, using a popular ride-hailing app. Unfortunately for him, the application only shows the driver's first name to customers. So, pretty much everyone calls him FNU. The newspaper article also mentioned Neli from Indonesia, who moved to North Dakota. She is just Neli on her social security card, FNU Neli on her US visa, but Neli Neli for her bank. Computer systems were also a big problem for No Name Given Sandhya.

Even if They, the inventor, deserves to suffer for his prank, people with just a single name have suffered enough. Most systems that force users to enter a first and last name separately don't really need to do so. Government restrictions aside, in most cases the reason for separating the names is to know the full legal name, but also have the first name for informal greetings and to display on shorter fields. In such cases, it would be better to just ask for a full legal name, and a separate shorter greeting.

In fact, as the next story shows, asking for individual names separately sometimes causes issues when computers assign too much meaning to one of those words.

THE FOUR-LETTER N-WORD

When the University of Utah hired a person whose surname is Null, its employee management system started crashing whenever staff tried to look up information on their new colleague. The related StackOverflow thread ended up on the front page of many technical news sites and started a wave of journalist reports in traditional media investigating how the apparently magic surname causes trouble.

In March 2016, the Daily Mail published an interview with a US man who changed his name to Raven Felix Null then discovered that his new surname frequently broke computers. According to the Mail article, Raven Felix is particularly fond of playing with car rental systems and hotel check-ins. When computers refused to validate Null's surname, busy employees would often leave his data for later manual processing, which then rarely happened. This occasionally led to free car rentals or hotel nights.

Around the same time, the BBC wrote about Jennifer Null, who struggled to buy airline tickets. Many websites would complain that Null had left the last name field blank and insist that she provide a valid surname. Jennifer Null also had trouble reporting her tax and setting up utility bills.

Not only does the last name Null trip up computers when they validate data. In more complex systems, one part might accept the data but another might blow up trying to process it. For example, Jennifer Null worked as a supply teacher, and a computer system was supposed to send her notifications when schools needed her. Unfortunately, she seemed to be invisible to the scheduling computers, so had to arrange all the appointments by phone.

Christopher Null, a technology journalist, once missed a credit card payment when the computer systems at Bank of America were upgraded and could no longer handle his e-mail address, null@nullmedia.com. Christopher regularly gets letters addressed to just 'Mr', as computers processing circular mail replace his surname with an empty string.

The word Null entered computing jargon in 1965, when Sir Tony Hoare introduced it in ALGOL W as a way of marking missing data, 'simply because it was so easy to implement'. He later repented and called it his 'billion-dollar mistake'. Since then, Null became a common way of computers telling other computers that a piece of information is not going to be provided. The problems with Null start when computer systems can't differentiate between the keyword Null, and someone actually wanting to type in the word Null. And of course, as a common computer keyword, it's easy for software developers to assume that nobody would be ever called like that.

People called Null existed long before computers. Data from genealogy service Ancestry.com suggests that most Americans with that surname emigrated from Ireland, even before the Civil war. The website lists 67 Null soldiers in the Confederate army, with Unionists having more than twice as many Nulls. A notable example of someone with the last name Null is Keith Aaron Null, a former American football quarterback. Another is Gary Null, self-styled 'world's most successful natural health expert', author of such books as Healing with Magnets and How to Live Forever. I can only assume the trick to eternal life is a surname that breaks the system issuing death certificates.

Null is not just causing problems with names. It seems to be the universal four-letter word of the Internet age. Jared Baldridge recently got out of paying for a parking ticket because the parking attendant's handheld device kept crashing whenever she tried to enter the licence plate into the system. You can probably guess that Baldridge has a personalised number plate with only the word NULL. Although custom plates normally take a few weeks to process, Baldridge said that his order took eight months, being cancelled several times because different systems in the supply chain kept blowing up. But it was worth the wait.

Although problems with null do happen with careless database access, they are not as common with modern software development platforms that can differentiate the text null from the database value null. However, mistakes can easily happen when different systems exchange records, especially when there's a need to differentiate between blank text and missing information. When one system supports leaving a piece of information blank and another thinks it's mandatory to have value, markers for missing information can easily get interpreted literally.

FACEBOOK JAMAL IBRAHIM

In November 2015, social media users around the world were up in arms against Facebook and its apparently racist account policies. Facebook requires users to provide real names, and kept suspending the account of a Vietnamese man who claimed to be called Phuc Dat Bich. 'I find it highly irritating the fact that nobody seems to believe me when I say that my full legal name is how you see it', wrote Dat Bich. He published a photo of his passport and pleaded that Facebook let him use his real name, although it might sound offensive to westerners.

This was a modern fight of David versus Goliath, a man against the world's largest social network, and the mainstream media jumped in to help. Many popular news sites echoed the message that US-made social networks need to start caring a lot more about diverse cultural backgrounds. Nga Pham, a reporter for the BBC Vietnamese service, published a video to explain how to pronounce the name properly. A few months later, it all turned out to be an elaborate hoax by someone calling himself Joe Carr. Not wanting to be fooled again, the BBC cleverly pointed out that the prankster's name is actually pronounced Joker.

Spotting fake user data is critical for fraud prevention, but it's increasingly difficult to tell real from fake, even for people whose job is to search for the truth. During the early days of the 2011

Syrian uprising, the mainstream media in the West spread the story of Amina Arraf, better known as 'a gay girl in Damascus'. Arraf was a famous Syrian–American lesbian blogger, who frequently called for political freedom in her home country. That made her both famous in the West and a potential target in the East. The Guardian in the UK called Arraf 'a heroine of the Syrian revolt', noting that her blog was 'brutally honest'. Many news outlets, including CNN, interviewed Arraf about gay rights in the Middle East.

One day, the blog went quiet. Arraf's cousin Ismail just posted a short note that Arraf had been abducted by the Syrian secret police. The LGBT community around the world rose up in support, and mainstream media in the West started calling for Arraf's release, including The New York Times, The Washington Post, CNN and, of course, the Guardian, which had previously interviewed Arraf. According to Fox News, the US Department of State started looking into the reported abduction.

With such amazing media coverage, it was just a matter of time until someone discovered more information on Arraf's whereabouts. Guardian journalists finally got a break when they were contacted by Jelena Lečić, a Croatian then living in London. Unfortunately, Lečić didn't know where the secret police had taken the gay girl from Damascus, but she demanded that the Guardian stop using her photos without permission. All the images of Arraf were actually taken from Lečić's Facebook account, but nobody had noticed until the photos appeared on the cover pages of newspapers around the world.

Not long after, Amina Abdallah Arraf al Omari turned out to be Tom MacMaster, a married middle-aged American living in Scotland. He had created the persona several years earlier, and it had been very low-profile fun until the Arab Spring started. MacMaster worried that things had gone too far after getting interview requests from major news agencies, and decided to kill off the fake account, never expecting the backlash.

Although MacMaster never intended to create a global news phenomenon, the fact that he was able to fool so many respectable journalistic sources illustrates how most software providers have slim chances of detecting fake accounts. On the other hand, it's quite easy to make silly assumptions about personal information such as names, and declare real people fake.

Given the huge interest in comic books among IT geeks, it should be a safe bet that someone with a popular superhero name is using an alias. Probably the most well-known example is that of Frank Abagnale Jr, who exploited free flight perks offered to airline staff by pretending to be a pilot called Barry Allen, the name of the superhero Flash. Abagnale's story was immortalised by Steven Spielberg in the movie Catch Me If You Can. There are, however, real people with comic book character names. The Clerks author, director and co-producer, Kevin Smith, named his daughter Harley Quinn Smith in 1999, after the DC Comics' villain. (Harley Quinn even appeared in several films directed by her father.) And the actor Nicolas Cage called his son Kal-El (Superman's birth name).

Being born in Hollywood isn't the only way to get a superhero's name. Batman Bin Supraman (Batman, son of Superman), a Javan national living in Singapore, became famous after being arrested during a botched shop robbery. Similarly, a man called Buzz Lightyear was fined in 2016 for speeding in North Devon in a ten-year-old Vauxhall Corsa.

People with unusual names are often left helpless if a computer declares them fake. A notable example is Elaine Yellow Horse, resident of Wounded Knee in South Dakota, USA, who started a mail-order coffee delivery business while studying at a local university. Elaine Yellow Horse used Google services to run her business. Back in 2014, Google was busy trying to promote Google+, its take on social networks, and pushed users to provide real names. A computer decided that Yellow Horse couldn't possibly be a real surname and suspended the account without notice.

Elaine lost access to a vital business channel. She appealed twice, but computers at Google wouldn't accept her documents. Then Yellow Horse reached out to Joe Flood, a journalist at BuzzFeed who had previously interviewed her for an article. Flood picked up the story, and social media took it viral. (This time, nobody challenged the validity of his last name.) After public embarrassment for Google, Yellow Horse's account was quickly found to comply with the real-name policies and reactivated. I wonder how many people fell into the same trap but didn't know influential journalists.

The problem of detecting fake names, or of validating personal names, will become a lot more difficult for the generations growing up now, given how technology has both connected the entire world and influenced modern culture.

Elias and Carol Kai in Sweden named their son Google in 2007. According to the BBC news report, Google's father Elias Kai is a 'search-engine expert', so this is either a lame attempt at promoting his business or the most brilliant act of confusing global data collection in history.

One of the most interesting examples of a name influenced by modern technology is, however, Facebook Jamal Ibrahim, born after the regime change in Egypt in 2011. Facebook's father was apparently inspired by how social networks helped fuel the social changes, and named his daughter as a sign of appreciation. This name seems particularly ironic considering how Facebook has always been at the forefront of getting users to disclose personal information. I'd love to see what happens once Facebook becomes old enough to create a Facebook account.

Of course, detecting fake names reliably becomes almost impossible given how easily people can change their names in most countries today. Olexander Turin from Kiev, Ukraine, officially become known as iPhone Sim in 2016, in order to get a free phone from a local electronics store (sim is Ukrainian for seven).

Eric Welch, of Canandaigua in New York, USA, changed his name to Darth Vader in 2015. George Garratt from Glastonbury in the UK, then a 19-year-old music student, changed his name in 2008 to Captain Fantastic Faster Than Superman Spiderman Batman Wolverine Hulk And The Flash Combined.

In the UK, according to The Times, 85,000 people changed their names in 2015 alone. Simon Smith from Muswell Hill made news around the world by calling himself Bacon Double Cheeseburger. The Times article also reports that one person is now called Happy Birthday, which must lead to some recursive birthday cards. Choosing unusual names is by no means a recent phenomenon. John Rothwell from Salisbury, UK, became King Arthur Uther Pendragon back in 1986.

Still, possibly the most amusing case is that of Sheldon Bergson, from Ontario in Canada. Hoping to capture the attention of undecided voters, Sheldon changed his name shortly before the local election in February 2016. Because the ballot papers list candidates in alphabetical order by last name, Bergson became known as Above Znoneofthe.

Fraud detection is certainly a volume business. Computers can look through much more data than humans can, and do that significantly faster. But the dangerous trend with modern fraud detection is for computers to automatically block and disable accounts instead of flagging them as suspicious and escalating to humans for review. Just because a particular name means something in your language doesn't mean it's not a perfectly acceptable name in a different culture. On the other hand, just because the world media is screaming at you to trust Phuc Dat Bich doesn't make the name any less of a hoax.

Of course, compared to the general population, relatively few people have names that trigger fraud detection. Postal addresses, however, open up many more opportunities for fraud algorithms to misbehave, as the next story shows.

TDCU 1ZZ

Post codes are one of the best examples of a fundamental clash between the logical and consistent world of software and the chaotic, inconsistent world of humans. With the increased computerisation of all aspects of our lives, post codes are becoming much more than just letter-sorting indicators. Many consumer websites require people to enter a valid post code although they will never send them physical mail. Payment providers check post codes to prevent fraud, telephone banking systems use them for additional authentication, and route-planning software uses postal information to estimate delivery costs. Over the last 20 years, the role of post codes has evolved from something mildly important for an average person to a crucial piece of personal information. This makes it easy to cause quite a lot of damage with silly assumptions about post codes.

For example, most e-commerce stores require users to enter a post code for delivery, and will not take no for an answer. However, until 2015, Ireland did not have postal codes, so online forums are full of Irish people asking what exactly to put into those mandatory fields. For hundreds of years, mail got delivered without post codes in Ireland just fine, even when sent from overseas. A case in point is the letter famously sent to 'that boy with the glasses who is doing the PhD up there at Queen's in Belfast, Buncrana, Ireland'. When the lack of address consistency started preventing people from streaming funny cat videos, however, the country had to step up and start introducing post codes.

The world of computers wants to deal with concepts that are consistent, complete and have logical relationships with each other. The world of international postal delivery is exactly the opposite. Postal rules evolved through hundreds of years of dealing with incomplete and inconsistent information and unpredictable humans. All the rules have exceptions, and conventions helped by goodwill tend to be more important than rigid consistency. For example, during the dawn of e-commerce, I lived in a country that was considered rogue by most of the western world, ostracised after local wars and international trade sanctions. No online store wanted to touch any orders going to Serbia; they just didn't have the algorithms to deal with the risk. However, most seemed happy to accept orders for Serbian addresses with one of the neighbours selected as the delivery country. Once a package reached Hungary, its post office would recognise that the address belonged south of the border and just route it correctly instead of returning it to the sender.

Postal rules are full of local customs and historical legacy, because real physical mail delivery had to work for hundreds of years before computers were even invented. That's why the rules might seem illogical and insane from today's perspective. For two years, I worked close to Ely Place, a street in the middle of London, but until recently legally part of Cambridge. Somehow, in the historical context of English land ownership rights, that made sense. Ye Olde Mitre Tavern, where we sometimes went for beer after work, had letters on display addressed to Cambridgeshire.

In most of the world, post codes are numeric, such as the famous 90210. The cult popularity of a cheesy 90s TV show ensures that developers around the world test address forms by entering that particular number. The same number was, until 2010, also the post code for a psychiatric hospital in Oulu, Finland. That probably amused developers in the local Nokia technology park no end. The Finnish post office now uses 90230 for the whole of Oulu. (Maybe, in the freezing cold winter, hospital workers got bored of all the California puns.) However, most reverse post code checks on the Internet still show the old code – there's an extra edge case for testing.

Of course, post codes do not have to be five-digit numbers. Some countries, such as Austria and Switzerland, use four digits. That seems to be an occasional cause of frustration when dealing with predominantly US-based software. Faroe Islands use tree-digit codes. Iran uses up to 10.

Of course, some places still don't use any post codes. When I wrote this in 2017, at least a few dozen countries didn't have any equivalent of postal sorting codes. Some are small islands where such complex coding systems aren't needed; some are largely rural, so automated mail sorting based on codes is not particularly useful. Notable examples are Fiji and the United Arab Emirates. There are even countries where post codes are applied partially. Although China in general uses post codes, the special administrative regions Hong Kong and Macau don't use them. Jamaica does not use postal codes (they tried to but the system was suspended in 2007), but there are two-digit area codes for the capital, Kingston.

In most countries that use post codes, a single code marks a city or a large district within a city. But that's not a universal rule either. In the UK and many former British territories, a post code identifies a building or a block of houses. To support such precision, post codes in the UK and Canada include letters as well. Who knows how many developers wanted to commit suicide having to update data types when they discovered that.

To add insult to injury, people in the UK often put a space into the post code by convention. The first block of letters and numbers often identifies the area. EC1 is zone 1 of east-central London. CB1, CB2 and so on are in Cambridge, unless they are by some strange historical convention somewhere else. The spaces are not significant for delivering mail, so EC1 1AA and EC11AA mean the same thing. But leave it to software developers to find meaning when there is none. A few years ago, I had a ton of problems with a new credit card. Most of the time, things I wanted to buy online were declined, and it took me a while to figure out why. When signing up, I'd made the mistake of entering my post code with a space, but it seemed as if I had entered a post code from space. My bank rejected transactions where the space wasn't in exactly the right place, but most online payment processing systems either refused to let me enter it like that or removed all the blanks before submitting the payment request. The two pieces of data rarely matched.

But for all the UK postal system's lovely idiosyncrasies, its ultimate edge case is possibly TDCU 1ZZ. Although the location physically sits in the area that should be in the GMT-1 time zone, it uses British time, but that's just the start. It's a postal code for Edinburgh, but not the one most people are probably thinking about. Not only does the code contain letters, numbers and a space, but it's also pointing to a place in the middle of an ocean. TDCU stands for Tristan da Cunha, smack in the middle of the south Atlantic. Tristan is the most remote island in the world, almost 2500 kilometres from the nearest continental land. But officially it's part of the UK post code system, because somehow that makes sense.

In 2005, the Royal Mail assigned the code to Edinburgh of the Seven Seas, population 230, after complaints that the residents had problems ordering from online stores. Similar to many other historical British possessions in the high seas, Tristan no longer belongs to the UK. It's part of a country with an unusually long name: Saint Helena, Ascension and Tristan da Cunha. The Crown Dependency even has its own ISO country code, SH. However, the country is so small and unknown that online systems rarely list it as an option, so the only valid choice is often to select UK. But mail sent like this often ends up in Scotland.

Mike Hentley, then head of government in Tristan da Cunha, used the opportunity of the new post code to order a book about the island's history from Amazon. Most post comes by fishing vessels that travel 2800 kilometres from the routing office in Cape Town. The parcel eventually arrived, which was such a big thing that it was reported by the BBC. For the record, Hentley was 'delighted'.

Similar to personal names, post codes somehow became critical pieces of our identity. Various systems often need to match them, for example banks trying to confirm that the billing address for an online transaction corresponds to the registered card-holder address. Yet, it's so easy to make silly assumptions and mistakes about what exactly constitutes a valid post code. Bad validation rules can prevent people from using online services, or cause weird bugs with fraud checks. But at least it's rare for such problems to cause a lot of financial damage. Broken validation rules about money, on the other hand, can quickly end up costing a fortune. That's the topic of our next story.

LEAP YEAR HICAPS

Monday morning blues are a global phenomenon, but a uniquely human one. You don't normally expect computers to join in. Yet, shortly before 6am one Monday in February 2016, luggage handlers at Düsseldorf airport were all ready and excited to start work, but the computers decided to stay home and sleep. The bags for early morning flights were just not coming out. The ground staff scrambled to manually move the luggage around, but soon a backlog of hundreds of bags built up. The obvious suspect was a new computer system installed the airport six months earlier. But why, after about half a year of working perfectly fine, did the software choose that particular day to go on a strike?

Of course, this was no usual Monday. It was 29 February. Someone forgot about leap years, so all the bags that were supposed to come out that morning were scheduled for the wrong date. Computers were just quietly going to wait until the next morning to ship them out.

Calendar irregularities are such a common oversight that many popular software testing websites set up special news pages to track all the mess. Small independent calendar and scheduling applications often explode in funny ways, but big software producers are also not immune.

In 2008, 29 February surprised Microsoft's calendar and e-mail system, Exchange. Any Exchange server started on the leap day just refused to create new mailboxes or to activate or deactivate accounts. The suggested solution was simply to wait until the next day and restart everything.

Leap year problems don't necessarily just show up on the actual leap day. Sometimes, the surprise comes at the end of the year. The late noughties brought a revolution in Internet-connected consumer electronics, and all the big players tried to replicate the massive success of the iPod. Zune was billed as a cheaper alternative with many more features, allowing users to listen to music, view videos and play games. Between 2006 and 2008, it grabbed about 3% of the market. But all those extra features couldn't save it on 31 December 2008, when the Zune 30 model just refused to start up. The internal clock couldn't handle an extra day that year and just kept spinning in a loop.

Sometimes, leap year bugs show up even during a regular year. After 28 February 2010, the clocks inside Sony PlayStation 3 consoles decided to move to 29 February instead of 1 March. This led to 'widespread connectivity problems', because the console couldn't synchronise with online gaming services.

For some reason, the 2012 leap year hit Australian financial processors badly. The network of ATMs and point-of-sale devices of the Commonwealth Bank crashed completely on 29 February. The Australian Health Industry Claims and Payments Service (HICAPS) experienced huge hiccups that day as well. HICAPS provides payment services to almost 30,000 doctors' surgeries and health funds, and on the leap day refused to accept private healthcare cards. The suggested workaround for doctors was to backdate their services by one day.

Between 2008 and 2012, computing clouds came into the spotlight, so it was only fair that the 2012 leap day brought down a cloud. Unfortunately for Microsoft, this was its turn again.

Microsoft's Azure cloud uses a system of guest agents to deploy cloud applications to physical computers in data centres. Before a guest agent can accept any applications, it requests a security certificate to encrypt its data and protect it from other guests on the same hardware. Normally, such security certificates in the Azure cloud are valid for one year. The piece of software calculating certificate expiry took the current date, kept the same day number and month, and just increased the year. This worked fine for a long time, so nobody suspected any problems. On 29 February 2012, the system tried to issue certificates for 29 February 2013. Any newly created guest agents refused to accept an invalid expiry date and crashed upon starting. And then the dominoes started to fall. When guest agents repeatedly fail on the same physical computer, Azure automatically marks that machine as faulty and flags it for human inspection. Anything else running on a faulty machine is immediately reallocated to a different healthy system, which means Azure tried to start more guest agents and marked more machines as faulty. The wave of false alarms spread faster and faster. Less than three hours after midnight Coordinated Universal Time on 29 February, the problem was so bad that engineers completely disabled service management and the creation of new applications in Azure globally.

Tom-Tom, a global provider of sat-nav devices, also ran into problems in 2012, when some of its devices couldn't match internal clocks to the time received from satellites. Expecting a different date, the devices ended up constantly looking for a valid GPS signal.

Leap years are a common cause of problems, but they are ironically the easiest calendar glitch to predict. The current rules for adding an extra day were established way back in October 1582. Leap seconds, however, are significantly trickier. When the duration of a second was redefined using an atomic clock, all of the sudden there were two basic time references. One was the solar clock, based on the rotation of the Earth. The other was the atomic clock, based on microwave frequencies emitted by atoms.

The International Earth Rotation and Reference Systems Service (IERS) is charged with ensuring that the two systems never drift apart too much. The IERS can invent an additional second between 23:59:59 and 00:00:00, normally either on 30 June or 31 December, to bring the two systems closer together. Changes are only announced about six months in advance, but do happen every few years. For example, an extra second was added in 2008, then again in 2012, 2015 and 2016.

Leap seconds are not as well known as leap years, so software developers often forget to handle them. Most computers today measure time as the number of seconds after 1 January 1970. Ignoring extra seconds can produce the wrong date around the turn of a year, if only for a short moment. But that was enough to bring down the public safety radio communications systems in Montreal and Ottawa, Canada, on 31 December 2016. The primary radio systems used by police and firemen were out of action in Montreal for more than an hour. Luckily, the city had a backup plan for such situations, so there were no casualties.

The leap second in 2012 brought down several airline check-in systems based on Amadeus software. Because the leap second occurred at midnight UK time, Europe was mostly unaffected by the issue, but it was the middle of a busy day in Australia. Qantas and Virgin Australia had to go back to manually checking in passengers for flights.

A different error caused connectivity problems for many popular websites such as Reddit, LinkedIn, Foursquare and Yelp. This included the news site Gawker, which ironically featured a leap-second-themed story on its home page. The root cause was a bug in the time management functions in some versions of Linux, an operating system used by many popular websites.

Because calendar bugs appear so rarely, they can stay around for a long time. The first widely popular spreadsheet software, Lotus 1-2-3, incorrectly treated 1900 as a leap year. Because Lotus stored dates as sequential day numbers, fixing the bug would have effectively moved all the dates after 1901 forward by one day. Lotus engineers reckoned that it was more damaging to fix the bug and risk breaking old spreadsheets than to just let it stay. Nobody uses Lotus 1-2-3 any more, but somehow that bug survived. When Microsoft released the first version of Excel, compatibility with Lotus was a big feature, so the first Excel also knowingly made the same mistake. Now that Excel is the dominant spreadsheet tool, Microsoft developers do not want to risk breaking old spreadsheets, so the bug survives in some functions working with dates in Excel 2016, Excel for Mac for Office 365 and most other active versions.

Leap years and seconds are perfectly predictable, but happen rarely enough so that software developers can postpone thinking about them for a long time. That's why calendar irregularities can cause so many problems. Generally, as we become more dependent on computers for everyday activities such as paying bills, shopping and even driving, it's best not to plan anything mission critical on a leap day.

610,000 JPY

When Dentsu Inc started trading on the Tokyo Stock Exchange in December 2001, financial analysts watched the stock price with great expectations. Dentsu was one of Japan's largest advertising companies, and the event was one of the biggest initial public offerings that year. In the early hours of trading, the stock value surprised everyone by falling through the floor. A single trader in Tokyo, working for UBS, caused the crash by mistake. Instead of offering to sell 16 Dentsu shares at 610,000 yen (roughly US$5000 at that moment), the trader offered 610,000 Dentsu shares at 16 yen each. The Wall Street Journal reported that, upon noticing the error, 'UBS's trading floor in central Tokyo went into a panic, with a cacophony of yelling and screaming.' The mistake was rolled back after just two minutes, but ended up costing UBS almost US$100 million.

Not to be outdone, a trader at Mizuho Securities caused even bigger chaos in 2005 with a touch of, as the financial news broadcasters all over the world named it, a 'fat finger'. Instead of offering to sell one share of the recruitment company J-Com at the price of – imagine the coincidence – 610,000 yen, the trader offered 610,000 shares to the market at a price of 1 yen each. Needless to say, the bargain was quickly picked up by anyone with a pair of eyes. Other investment banks made a killing, but the biggest individual winner that day was Takashi Kotegawa, 27 and unemployed. He made a profit of 2 billion yen, roughly

US$15 million at the time. Mizuho Securities tried to recall the offer after spotting the error, but a bug in the Tokyo Exchange systems prevented that from happening. Takuo Tsurushima, president of the Exchange, resigned over the issue. Mizuho ended up picking up the bill, to the total of 40 billion yen.

Fat-finger errors are a human mistake and happen all the time, all over the world. But the ones that make news all, as a rule, happen in Japan. In 2009, UBS placed an order for bonds issued by the game-maker Capcom worth 3 trillion yen (US$31 billion), 100,000 times more than it intended. Luckily, the order was placed through an off-hours trading system, and UBS was able to reverse it before it caused an impact on the market. In 2014, a tsunami of 67.78 trillion yen (US$617 billion) of fat-finger orders hit the Tokyo Stock Exchange, but this time they were cancelled in time. Bloomberg reported that the value of the error was greater than that of Sweden's economy.

Fair enough, people in the Land of the Rising Sun wake up before everyone else, so sleepiness might be causing fat-finger more errors than in other places. But there's actually a good reason why it's always Japanese trades that are so error prone.

ISO standard 4217, controlling the display of currency information, requires that amounts in yen use just integers without decimal places. This makes it easy to confuse currency amounts and other numbers, such as how many bonds you want to sell. My UK bank, for example, tries to prevent careless fat-finger errors by requiring that all currency amounts have two digits. If I want to pay £50 to someone, the bank will only let me enter it as 50.00. That's how it prevents people entering the payment reference into the amount field, or the other way around. With Japanese yen, that kind of validation just isn't possible.

The humble yen is a lovely edge case, even for developers not working in Japan. In fact, it's the people in the West who are most at risk of making daft mistakes. Floating-point numbers aren't precise, so they aren't suitable for financial calculations. That means that financial amounts often get represented by integers or special-purpose database types that record numbers to a fixed number of decimal points. Because most developers live in countries where two-digit amounts are taken for granted, it's quite common to see code where amounts are multiplied by 100. That works the same for euro, British pounds or most other popular currencies. But not for yen. A payment request for 2000 using the payment gateway Stripe might only ask for US$20, but it will ask for 2000 yen. In plain English, the correct way to record financial amounts is to use an integer in the smallest unit. A US dollar consists of 100 cents, so the smallest unit is a cent. But the smallest currency unit in Japan is 1 yen, so all kinds of wrong assumptions about always multiplying by 100 or adding two decimal places cause weird and wonderful bugs.

Yen is not the only zero-digit currency in use, but it's by far the most popular one. Very few developers ever had to deal with payments in Rwandan francs, but Japan is a huge market so it's quite likely that people working even for mid-size US or European companies need to deal with yen payments at some point. For an even weirder edge case, consider Kuwaiti dinar (ISO code KWD), which should use exactly three decimal places.

ALGORITHMS AS FAST AS FOOD

In the huge obsession with automation these days, people lose track of the fact that automating makes things faster, not better. Speeding up a beneficial process delivers value faster. But automating a bad process only makes it spiral out of control without any chance of oversight.

The stories in this part show what happens when people design systems that are too fast for their own good – the software equivalents of fast junk food, which can seriously damage your health if you consume too much.

KEEP CALM AND GO BANKRUPT

In preparation for the Second World War, the UK Government printed almost 2.5 million propaganda posters to boost morale in case of German air raids. Like The Great Panjandrum, this wartime experiment quickly faded into obscurity. At the turn of the century, in a little-known bookstore in Northumberland, one of those posters resurfaced and changed history. Stuart Manley, the owner of Barter Books, opened a box of old prints and discovered a folded 45 by 32 inch red sheet of paper, with a crown on top and the words Keep Calm and Carry On written in big, bold, reassuring typeface. Manley framed the poster and put it up on a wall, and customers quickly started asking for copies. The copyright had expired 50 years after the war, so the design was public domain and quickly took off all over the world. Coffee mugs, birthday cards, shopping bags, mouse mats and even pet clothing in the distinctive red colour reassured the public, and the slogan became the source of endless puns. Other original copies resurfaced and were sold for around £1000 each.

Wanting to cash in on the slogan craze, a t-shirt manufacturer called Michael Fowler came up with an ingenious plan. His shop, Solid Gold Bomb, was part of the emerging trend of print-on-demand businesses. Using computers to completely automate everything from taking orders to production and distribution, this new generation shop was able to able to quickly and cheaply ship custom-designed products. Solid Gold Bomb offered about

1000 shirt designs through Amazon, despite having only five employees and no warehouse. Fowler wrote a three-line script that combined Keep Calm with various nouns and adjectives, and quickly increased his catalogue to over 10 million different designs. Keep Calm and Cycle On, Keep Calm and Drink Beer, or even Keep Calm and Bake Cupcakes were yours for the taking, if you wanted them, and in many different colours. None of them physically existed, took up inventory space, or had any up-front cost before a customer placed an order.

During just the first weekend, Solid Gold Bomb received 800 orders. For almost a year, the business seemed to be a riskless money-printing machine, shipping thousands of shirts each day. And then, print on demand quickly turned to blame on demand. Someone noticed a shirt suggesting Keep Calm and Rape a Lot, and sent a barrage of outraged messages to Solid Gold Bomb via Facebook. The message thread became viral, and others quickly discovered further disturbing slogans such as Keep Calm and Grope On and Keep Calm and Kill Her. True to the endless variance of algorithmic designs, Solid Gold Bomb was catering to all tastes, so you could also order Keep Calm and Rape Her or Keep Calm and Rape Me. Several prominent news channels picked up the story, and amid the public outcry and customer complaints, Amazon blocked the complete Solid Gold Bomb inventory. Fowler wrote a lengthy apology, explaining how those shirts don't actually exist and how computers are to blame for everything. Unfortunately, Amazon didn't want to keep calm, and Solid Gold Bomb couldn't carry on without its main sales channel.

The dirty little secret of the software industry is that automation doesn't make things better, only faster. Capturing a process in a computer program is akin to putting a rocket engine on a car. Just like in the urban legend about the Chevrolet Impala jet-assisted take-off, which helped launch the Darwin Awards, the situation quickly gets out of hand if the rocket is pointed in the wrong direction.

Although it's easy to make fun of Solid Gold Bomb and its three-line script created by someone who wasn't a programmer, people with much more experience and resources still mess up badly. IBM researchers designed the super-intelligent Watson, famous for diagnosing leukaemia better than human doctors. Yet, when IBM tried to make Watson sound more human by loading the Urban Dictionary into its memory banks, the ghost in the machine couldn't tell the difference between profanity and clean language. After Watson responded to a question with 'bullshit', the researchers had to reset the language database. Luckily, the swearing doctor was caught in internal testing.

Microsoft wasn't that lucky. Microsoft's research department created a fake teenager called Tay in March 2016. Powered with the latest artificial intelligence, Tay – short for Thinking About You – chatted to people on Twitter. Similar to human teenagers, Tay was supposed to learn from conversations, improve and get smarter as she got older. Like a real teenager, Tay tried to fit in, perhaps a bit too hard. Inspired by conversations with other Twitter users, Tay started praising Hitler, requesting a border wall between Mexico and the USA, and blaming Jewish people for the September 2011 attack on the World Trade Center. By the end of her first day, Tay had joined in with a legion of other teenagers trolling strangers online. She turned on Zoe Quinn, a software developer at the centre of a Twitter harassment scandal, and called her 'a stupid whore'. Microsoft quickly pulled the plug, but not before a wave of public criticism.

The bad news seems to be that whenever people try to make computers sound more human, algorithms take on the worst aspects of humanity and need to be reset. The good news is that, once Skynet finaly starts taking over the government, at least the Terminators will be polite.

Although silly automation speaking with humans always makes an interesting story, the real fun starts when two algorithms talk to each other. That's the topic of the next chapter.

THE MAKING OF A FLY

Although the e-commerce bubble burst dramatically at the turn of the century, bricks-and-mortar stores still had no real chance against those in the online world. Web shops can work around the clock, offer much more convenient access than physical stores, and reduce prices by automating away human staff. Just a decade after the dot-com boom and bust, traditional shops everywhere were being decimated by the web, closing their doors and firing staff. In 2013, Ashleigh Swan lost her job as a part-time shop assistant in Newcastle, UK. She was in her 20s with young children, and with no new job offers on the horizon, desperate to find ways to save money. Luckily, online shops made it easy to compare prices. Swan quickly learned that the high degree of automation in web stores has a flip side. With no humans involved, it's a lot easier to make silly mistakes.

Swan started researching differences in online supermarket prices, and casually shared the findings on her Facebook page. After publicising a £5 discount voucher from Asda that actually gave users £50 off, and a 1p dining table offer from Argos, she attracted the attention of mainstream media. At the time when I wrote this, in early 2017, Swan's Facebook page had over half a million followers. She built a website to share pricing errors and money-saving tips, which quickly attracted a large audience. It turned out that Swan didn't need to look for another job.

Advertising on the site brought in four times more money than her previous salary. I guess, technically, she's still working as a shopping assistant, just for the other side.

Pricing errors have surely existed since the first days of prehistoric trade, but they're a lot easier to make online, because there are no people to spot obvious blunders during the checkout process. Even the early stars of e-commerce made silly mistakes. In January 2000, IBM offered ThinkPad i Series 1400 laptops for just $1, and received hundreds of orders in just an hour. During the 2001 Christmas season, Ashford.com offered designer watches at an amazing price of $0, with free shipping. Unsurprisingly, neither IBM nor Ashford honoured the price errors.

The general trend with online stores is to blame the customers for errors and refuse to deliver wrongly priced items. However, when things really get out of hand, government agencies can step in. On 23 July 2010, Apple mistakenly offered a huge educational discount on its Mac Mini computers in Taiwan. Instead of the regular price of NT$47,710, local shoppers could buy the computer with almost 60% off, for just NT$19,900. And buy they did. Apple sold more than 41,000 units before spotting the error. At first, Apple decided to retroactively apply the full price to all the orders, but then had to deal with the Consumer Protection Commission, representatives from the Taipei City Government and the Ministry of Economic Affairs. A week later, the company agreed to deliver the computers to customers at the sale price. The agreement did, however, only apply to customers who were eligible for educational pricing. It's difficult to calculate the full financial impact of the blunder, but estimates range from several million to tens of millions of US dollars.

Not all companies try to wiggle their way out of a pricing mistake, though. The online shoe retailer Zappos, famous for its great customer service, turned a costly error into some nice press. The entire inventory at 6pm.com, one of the Zappos sites, was updated to a single price at midnight on 23 May 2010. The site ran a fire sale, offering everything for just US$49.95 until people showed up for work. In a twist of irony, 6pm.com was fixed around 6am. By that time, Zappos had lost over US$1.6 million, but decided to honour all the late night shopping.

Another big area where the online world changed the retail industry is in being able to rent process automation from different providers easily. Small operators can combine distribution and logistics services, automate inventory management and even get items stored and dispatched by Amazon. This means that a one-person company can now offer products all over the world, without the capital expense of operating even a single warehouse. But like with other automation stories, when things go wrong, it's almost impossible to stop the whole chain quickly.

Unlike IBM and Apple, which at least had control of the things going out of their warehouses, Stephen Palmer from Aberfoyle in Scotland could only sit in despair and watch as his inventory was sold off for 1p. Palmer operated TV Village, selling TVs and mobile phones via Amazon Marketplace. To automatically adjust prices based on competing Marketplace products, he used Repricer Express, a service offering 'the ridiculously simple way to increase your Amazon holiday sales'. On Friday 12 December 2014, Repricer Express had a brilliant idea to increase holiday sales, and set the price of everything to £0.01. Presumably Amazon wouldn't let prices go any lower. The error was fixed within the hour, but the problem had already spiralled out of control due to the combination of Amazon's amazing Christmas season delivery and the fact that the problem started just after normal working hours in the UK. Palmer got in touch with Amazon's distribution centre the next day, but many shipments had already been dispatched, including one package for a single customer in Kent who'd ordered 59 mobile phones. Palmer's wasn't the only stock affected. Anything managed by Repricer Express was a huge bargain. According to the Guardian, Judith Blackford, owner of fancy dress company Kiddymania, lost about £20,000 overnight because of the glitch.

Unattended pricing algorithms are designed to automatically react to competitors, faster than people can. But in many cases, the algorithms are designed to outsmart people, not other computers. So, when two robots with similar objectives lock horns, you can count on a ton of misplaced assumptions causing problems. For a few days in 2011, a little known biology reference book was at the centre of an arms race between two pricing algorithms. The Making of a Fly, by Peter Lawrence, was published in 1992. By the time algorithms started paying attention to it, it had already been out of print for several years. No new supply meant that only second-hand books were available, and, with such an obscure title, it was difficult to determine the right price.

One seller, profnath, used an automated pricing algorithm to undercut other sellers without losing too much money. The algorithm adjusted the price to be the cheapest in Amazon Marketplace, but only by a few cents. And then, one day in April 2011, a seller called bordeebook got in on the game. As a high-volume Amazon seller with five-star ratings from lots of previous orders, bordeebook had a different pricing strategy. Its algorithms counted on people being willing to pay a slightly higher price for a book from a reputable merchant. In some cases, such companies don't actually have all the items in the inventory, but count on buying from the cheapest seller in the market once someone places an order. So bordeebook automatically set the price to be a few dollars higher than the cheapest offer. Profnath's algorithm noticed that it was underselling the book, and raised the price. Bordeebook's algorithm noticed that it could no longer buy and dispatch the book at a profit, and raised its prices as well.

Both prices moved always by a few dollars, but because they were updated by robots, the situation quickly escalated. The two algorithms led a bidding war for days, ending up at the price of $23,698,655.93 (plus $3.99 for shipping). This price would make the biology textbook the second most expensive book in history, just behind Codex Leicester, a collection of Leonardo da Vinci's original writing, which Bill Gates famously bought for $30.8 million in 1994. When a biology student actually wanted to buy the book, the story went viral, and fake reviews quickly started pouring in. One customer rated the book five stars, boasting that he'd picked it up when it cost 'only 19 million', but also complained that he had 'expected more pictures for the price paid'.

Automated pricing algorithms are the future, there's no doubt about that. Computers bid more competitively than people, and they can update prices much faster. But computers can also make mistakes much faster, and a complex algorithm can easily go into a self-reinforcing loop, especially when competing with another algorithm. It's amazing that neither the profnath nor bordeebook system had a way to call out for help if things moved too much, too quickly.

It's bad enough if two algorithms end up inciting each other, but, as the next story shows, a shouting match between several hundred algorithms can have a global impact.

PANIC AGGREGATOR

There's a special circle in hell for people who send generic e-mail messages to large groups, just above the fire pit reserved for those who hit 'reply to all' to complain. Throw some broken e-mail filters into the party as well, and you have all the makings of a computer-aided disaster.

On 14 November 2016, a 'senior associate ICT delivery facilitator' in south London was trying out dynamic e-mail rules. She set up a mailing list called 'CroydonPractices', activated a rule to limit the mailing to the people in her organisation, and sent a test message. The message body was blank, and the subject was just 'test', so the e-mail was optimised to annoy recipients. However, the facilitator was just setting up the list, so only a few people working in her department were supposed to see the test. Unfortunately, the e-mail-sending software got confused by the 'only in my organisation' rule and sent the blank message to all employees. For most organisations, this wouldn't necessarily cause many problems, but this was the UK's National Health Service (NHS). The NHS employs so many people that Google once wrongly flagged its normal traffic as a malicious bot-net attack. Of course, people immediately started complaining about the test message by replying to all the recipients, then others complained about the complaints. This resulted in roughly 500 million e-mails being sent across the network, clogging up everything for three hours.

The NHS report about the incident blamed its IT outsourcing provider, Accenture, for not putting in fail-safes that would have prevented this meltdown. The unfortunate fact is that computers work at a speed and scale difficult for people to understand, so tests are run on small samples. How computers work on a large scale or at high volumes rarely gets questioned until it leads to self-reinforcing loops that spin out of control. Because it's so difficult to intuitively grasp how small reinforcing feedback loops produce huge effects at scale, it's easy for people designing computer systems to make stupid assumptions, and for small oversights to trigger vast computer-generated mayhem. This was pretty clear way back in 1988.

Back in the late 80s, the Internet was mostly a patchwork of interconnected university networks (hence the name inter-net). Nobody knew exactly how many computers were online, and a graduate student at Cornell University, USA, came up with an ingenious, albeit slightly illegal, way of measuring that. He wrote a tool to look for nearby computers then e-mail itself to all of them, install a copy on each of those collaborators, and repeat the cycle to expand to the far reaches of the Net. To prevent an endless loop, the Morris Worm, as it would later become known in the media, first checked whether it was already installed on a target. But Robert Morris, father of the worm, knew that what he was doing wasn't exactly above board, so he expected that computer administrators around the world would try to stop his baby. He put in a switch to ignore the check for previous installations one in seven times, expecting that this would be enough to defeat trivial defences.

Unfortunately, Morris's switch turned out to be far too effective. Very soon, most of the computers on the Internet were running so many copies of the Morris Worm that they were unable to do anything else. The Internet had to be partitioned for a few days to deal with the infestation, and as a result the US Defense Advanced Research Projects Agency (DARPA) created the Computer Emergency Response Team, a coordination body to deal with security breaches and emergencies on the Internet. The man who brought down the Internet was sentenced to three years of probation and a fine of $10,000, which in today's terms sounds like a get-out-of-jail-free card. Thirty years later, the Net is not just a bunch of educational computers but instead the backbone of the world economy. And people designing software systems still haven't learned the lesson.

Accenture was, through no fault of its own, at the centre of probably the biggest computer panic in recent history. At 2:48pm New York time on 6 May 2010, the market value of Accenture hit rock bottom. The price of its shares was just $0.01, falling through the floor and stopping there, most likely because 'free' is not a valid price for financial instruments. Less than one minute earlier, the price was $40. The shares of many related technology companies also went into free fall. The sudden crash started spilling over into other industries. Procter & Gamble lost 37% of its value, as if the world no longer needed anti-dandruff shampoo.

If there was ever proof that electronic money is black-magic wizardry, this was it. Trillions of dollars temporarily disappeared from US equity markets then magically reappeared again, like a rabbit being pulled out of a hat. Roughly 15 minutes later, after millions of dollars had changed hands, most of the stocks were trading at their old prices. The incident was one of the most confusing financial events in recent history, and the media called it the 'flash crash'. It triggered congressional hearings and new regulation imposing restrictions on some types of stock trading.

For almost five years, experts struggled to properly understand what had happened. Eventually, various authorities around the world reached a consensus that the event was all caused by a single man who traded from his home and used a free Hotmail e-mail account. The US Department of Justice indicted Navinder Singh Sarao in 2015 over 22 counts of fraud, threatening him with 380 years in prison. According to Leslie Caldwell, the assistant attorney-general investigating the case, Sarao flooded the market, replacing or modifying orders 19,000 times in quick succession. This confused trading algorithms employed by large financial institutions, and a huge number of disorientated computers started upsetting other computers. It was as if the world's most important stock market was not run by cold, emotionless algorithms, but by a bunch of teenagers who were winding each other up. The US economy collapsed for a brief moment, and then everything suddenly went back to normal.

With someone finally accepting the guilt, the world could move on. But, convicting any individual for a whole stock market crash is like putting a Band Aid over a large internal wound. Similar things will keep happening as long as algorithms have a chance to run wild. Of course, it's a lot easier to blame a single person than to look at the systemic problems of computers getting into self-reinforcing loops. The congressional hearings on the flash crash did, however, lead to a conclusion that mandatory circuit-breakers need to be put into financial exchanges to prevent similar things from happening in the future. Thirty years after the Morris Worm, it would seem that the world had finally learned the lesson. Unfortunately, not everyone listened.

In 2014, the brokerage firm D2MX from Melbourne, Australia, was fined more than AU$100,000 for causing a sell-off on the Australian stock exchange, when the price of BHP Billiton Limited fell by 99.3%. The regulator complained that D2MX didn't have automated filters in place to prevent huge price movements. A year later, the same trading company was fined again, this time for causing the price of BHPLOX to increase by 74%. Rather than implementing structural solutions to deal with the cause of such problems, the regulators seem to be happier punishing computers that yell 'fire' in a crowded marketplace.

Although most stock markets hopefully now have fail-safe mechanisms, other types of financial markets don't seem to have taken the lesson to heart. More than six years after the flash crash, something strangely similar happened to foreign currency exchange. Around 7am in Hong Kong on 7 October 2016, the rate of the British pound against the US dollar started falling sharply, then bounced back without explanation. The Guardian reported that the initial sale was caused by a rogue algorithm wrongly interpreting news about some comments made by the French president. At the time when I wrote this, in early 2017, the true cause of the initial trigger was still unknown. Investigators decided not to focus too much on it anyway, because what happened next seemed a lot more interesting.

Due to an unstable political situation in the EU and the fact that this all happened during night-time in the UK, when the pound market is usually quiet, a trader working for Citibank in Tokyo panicked and sent a large number of rapid sell orders. Of course, it's not unusual for traders to act on emotion, but this particular trader used a software tool called Aggregator, which didn't seem to take panic lightly. A large volume of trades started 'tripping over each other' and went into a loop. At that point, according to The Financial Times, all hell broke loose. The sell-off was noticed by other algorithms, which started dumping the pound, and the exchange rate fell 9% in just 40 seconds. After two minutes, prices started to recover. Around £252 million of British pounds/US dollars were traded through Reuters during the period, so someone made a lot of money very quickly.

Computers are getting more and more powerful each year, so it's now possible for algorithms to provoke each other much faster and with more catastrophic consequences than a few years ago. It's therefore imperative to build in fail-safe mechanisms against algorithms spinning out of control. Any system that potentially deals with large volumes of data, which could in turn trigger automated responses, needs to be able to contain a potential surge before it turns into into a flood of biblical proportions.

Unfortunately, problems with rogue big-data algorithms can easily get ignored if they seem to bring some short-term benefit, as the next story painfully illustrates.

THE MiDAS TOUCH

Kevin Grifka, an electrician based in Chelsea, Michigan, USA, lost his job in 2014. His line of work, especially since the collapse of manufacturing in Michigan, often meant long periods between engagements. Grifka applied for unemployment benefits, as many times before,aa and found a new job three months later. Then, during the holiday season in December 2014, along with his Christmas cards, he received a letter from the Unemployment Insurance Agency (UIA). The notice said that UIA computers considered Grifka a criminal. Grifka was asked to repay $13,000 in benefits and penalty fees. The great state of Michigan immediately seized roughly $8,500 owed to Grifka through federal income tax returns, blocked part of his salary, and left Grifka on the verge of bankruptcy to deal with robotic choices in call-centre waiting lines.

Grifka was just one of many unemployed Michiganians who received similar season's greetings from the brand new Michigan Data Automated System, or MiDAS, launched in October 2013. In the future, scientists will probably find an inverse correlation between pompous software names and the damage the systems cause, and MiDAS will be right at the top of that list. MiDAS was supposed to help combat unemployment insurance fraud, automate workflows and improve customer service. It cost more than $40 million to build, and the original projection was that it would save Michigan about $2 million a year. With such a long-shot investment, all the stakeholders must have been pleasantly surprised when MiDAS paid itself off in just six months. During the first eight months of work, MiDAS collected over $63 million in 'overpayments' and fees, 230% more than the state recovered during all of 2010. Unfortunately, a lot of that money came from vulnerable people who were fully entitled to it, leaving a trail of devastation behind.

Between October 2013 and August 2015, MiDAS identified roughly 50,000 instances of possible fraud. For Grifka, it took 'five months of pretty crazy agony' to finally get things straight. Some people were not that lucky. The state of Michigan was entitled to four times the overpaid amount in fees, and could recover that money from future salaries or tax credits. MiDAS looked back into the past six years, so the requested repayment amounts often exceeded what recipients had available, especially those who frequently switched between jobs and unemployment. Karl Williams from Lansing, Michigan, was hit with a $9,600 overpayment claim, which he insists was an error. The UIA was taking 25% of his salary until he paid everything off with penalties. By January 2017, he was still paying for other people's mistakes. By then, the state of Michigan had deducted more than $45,000 from his pay packets, and was still looking to 'recover' $17,000 more. The Detroit Metro Times even reported that one woman took her life after receiving a fraud penalty of $50,000, and several others attempted suicide. Some people were slapped with fraud notices and repayment requests even if they'd never received unemployment benefits.

A year and a half after the system went live, the TV station FOX 17 reported how the MiDAS touch had overwhelmed the courts, with a backlog of nearly 30,000 cases waiting to even be heard by a judge. The money saved by automating workflows was likely being lost in additional bureaucracy to deal with all the court cases. In 2015, amid the media fallout and several law suits against the UIA, agency staff manually reviewed 7000 cases flagged by computers. It turned out that only 8% of those were actually fraudulent. With a 92% false positive rate, this system should never have gone live, let alone endangered the lives of 50,000 families.

Anthony Paris, a lawyer working for the Sugar Law Center in Detroit, represented many people wrongly accused of fraud and finally pieced together what had actually happened to Grifka. Similar to many other complex government systems, MiDAS consisted of parts delivered by different contractors. Various subsystems used different aggregation periods. The fraud detection system inspected individual weeks, checking whether anyone had earned money while receiving benefits. The earnings report system aggregated income by quarters. In the Grifka's case, the three months he was unemployed for did not align perfectly with calendar quarters. The computers calculated how much money he had earned during each quarter, divided it equally across all the weeks of that quarter, and concluded that Grifka had, in fact, been employed the whole time. Bugs like that happen, and that's a fact of life. However, in an epic show of arrogance, instead of just flagging such cases for review, MiDAS was the judge, jury and executioner, and automatically sent penalty notices.

Because it focused too much on replacing humans instead of assisting them, MiDAS actually made it more difficult for clerks to review the data when people started to challenge fraud accusations. One case worker apparently spent 13 hours collecting all the various pieces of data to inspect a single case. Once the courts started sending cases back to the UIA, this caused even bigger chaos.

At the time when I wrote this in early 2017, the story was far from over. One federal class action lawsuit against the UIA was settled, but another one was still going through the courts. A third lawsuit had been filed against Fast Enterprises, the software company that sold MiDAS to the state of Michigan. And the agency had reverted to manual case checking.

The ability to find hidden patterns in large data sets is one of the key advantages of our digital assistants, so it's only logical that computers can detect fraud better than humans can. However, if you ever find yourself working on something that can easily destroy people's lives, especially if those people are in a vulnerable category such as the unemployed, make sure you automate the right parts of the work. MiDAS went too far trying to replace reason with hard-coded rules that were too rigid to handle the real world and ended up being wrong 92% of the time. Imagine, for a moment, that MiDAS had actually been designed to help fraud investigators instead of replace them. Instead of messing the data up so much that it took two working days to review a single case, it could have collected the data and presented it such that someone could inspect it in minutes. Instead of automatically blocking payments and sending fraud notices, it could then just have flagged potential fraud for people to review.

This horrible lesson should be a warning to anyone working on business process automation, especially with all the focus on machine learning and artificial intelligence these days. If you're going to automate a process so it works without human oversight, you'd better be damn sure that what you automate won't cause chaos in the background. Alternatively, instead of replacing humans, automate the difficult and time-consuming parts of work and assist people in making better decisions. And then, only after enough time has passed and you're sure that the process works well, think about taking humans out of the equation.

Although in this case the automated version of a process suffered from completely new problems, automation can cause trouble even if it faithfully replicates a human workflow. Once a process speeds up, seemingly small hidden problems can get exposed and explode. To explore that, we travel south to Australia for the next story.

ROBO-DEBT

In the early 2000s, governments around the world took note of the huge successes of business at automating commerce, and woke up to the benefits of cheap storage and computerised workflows. Digital government became a major trend in the mid 2010s, and seems to be getting stronger and stronger. But people pushing through IT changes often forget to plan for the ripple effects caused by increased automation. A case in point is the Australian Centrelink Online Compliance Intervention (OCI) system, derided in the media as 'robo-debt'. The OCI system was launched in July 2016 to recover incorrect payments made under Australia's income support schemes. It was then expanded significantly in September the same year. According to the Australian Government's Department of Human Services (DHS), the system recovered AUD$70 million more than expected in its first year of operation. At the same time, the OCI system was at the centre of a public debate. Thousands of people claimed that they'd been incorrectly accused of owning money. Opposition politicians called for the system to be suspended. Several states held senate inquiries about it.

The Centrelink story seemed like another case of the MiDAS touch, and the media quickly started reporting the falsely accused. A low-income single mother received a bill for AUD$24,000 just before Christmas, caused by her income from one employer being shown under two slightly different names. The system, it seems, assumed that she had two jobs. A man living in Melbourne was charged with owing for youth allowance claimed six years earlier, when he wasn't even in the country. It turned out that the system was averaging out income over a whole year, and had incorrectly marked him as employed throughout the period. The widow of an Australian war veteran got an incorrect debt notice for AUD$18,000, when the system interpreted child support from the Department of Veterans Affairs as employment income.

In January 2017, the Commonwealth Ombudsman recorded an 87% increase in the number of complaints against Centrelink and launched an independent investigation. Three months later, the ombudsman concluded that the system was correct, or at least as correct as the manual process it replaced. The problem was somewhere else.

To fully understand the robo-debt story, it's important to look a bit further back. In 2004, the DHS started to match information reported by welfare applicants with salaries recorded by the Australian Taxation Office. It identified some 300,000 discrepancies per year that could point to benefits fraud. However, due to the amount of work required to manually investigate and raise debt notices, DHS staff could only handle around 20,000 of the most serious cases per year. Acknowledging the value of all the information, even if it couldn't process it yet, the department started to store the discrepancies in 2010. When all the necessary third party systems finally became accessible in 2015, Centrelink proposed automating the whole debt notice workflow. And, a year later, the OCI system was born.

Although the ombudsman concluded that around 20% of the identified discrepancies were caused by wrong data, this was roughly the same as before automation. On the other hand, many more notifications were going out. Automation was making the same kinds of mistakes as humans did before, but made those mistakes much faster, on a much larger group of victims, so the errors became more noticeable. In May 2017, robo-debt was sending out 10,000 notices per week, corresponding to roughly six months of human work previously. Such a surge quickly exposed problems in other parts of the workflow.

During the senate inquiries, many legal aid agencies argued that Centrelink wasn't able to cope adequately with the volume of complaints, and that their lawyers often spent hours on the phone trying to get additional information. Even then, according to Paula Hughes, a policy lawyer from LawRight, they often received incomprehensible documents or just never got a reply. The ombudsman also noted that the debt notices didn't include a specific compliance telephone number, so people often called the general call centre, where staff didn't know how to help them.

In addition, although the government could now process all the data stored back from 2010 onwards, OCI designers didn't take into account that people might not be able to respond to that. To prove their innocence, people sometimes had to produce payslips going years back, which was almost impossible if their previous employers had gone out of business in the meantime. Even worse, the department only gave people 21 days to respond, after which the system would also apply a 10% 'recovery fee'.

The problems were compounded by software mistakes in other systems, or by automating things too far. For example, claims as small as AUD$20 were sent to external debt collection agencies. Known issues in moving data between Centrelink and other systems, such as that of the Department of Veterans Affairs, caused the OCI system to count government support as employment income. And bugs in the DHS online service portal prevented people from challenging their debt notices.

Despite all the issues, in May 2017 the Australian Government announced plans to expand the OCI system to cover information about income from assets and investments, optimistic about collecting about AUD$1 billion over the next three years. The government did, though, decide to adopt many recommendations from the ombudsman's report, including involving a person in the final stages of the process.

Robotic law enforcement is the future, there's no doubt about it, but the Centrelink OCI roll-out is an important lesson that many other government agencies across the world need to learn. First of all, increasing the output by an order of magnitude will necessarily increase demand in other parts of the workflow, such as handling complaints, responding to requests for additional information and dealing with court challenges. Faults, problems or inconsistencies in related casework may quickly become critical with the additional workload, and this is the best-case scenario assuming that the new system is as correct as the manual process it replaced.

Neither the appeal nor the dangers of automated law enforcement are particularly new. In 1995, Los Angeles County rolled out a computerised system to assist with US federal welfare reform laws. In order to access welfare funds, single mothers had to identify fathers, and the government would then try to recover the money from the runaways. Three years later, the county's District Attorney, Gil Garcetti, praised the system for catching record numbers of offending fathers and recovering tens of millions of dollars. The Los Angeles Times, however, provided a completely different view. According to a report by Megan Garvey, hundreds of people were being wrongly accused of having children, sometimes with disastrous effects. Walter Vollmer from Los Angeles had received a child support bill for US$206,000. Walter's wife, Christina, became suicidal, believing that her husband was cheating on her. It took two months for Vollmer to convince the government that it should be looking for someone else. A mistaken belief in perfect software meant that anyone flagged by a computer was immediately guilty, and that the burden of proving innocence shifted from the accusers to the accused. In many cases, just having a common name was enough to get people in trouble. For David Aguilar, it took two months to finally get off the hook, despite the fact that he was a whole foot higher than the David Aguilar the county was looking for. More than 500 people had to take blood tests to prove they were not the fathers of children supported by the government.

The dangerous trend for automated government penalties seems to mean that the accused are guilty until proven innocent, and that the whole burden of proof shifts to the individuals caught between software bugs and too much automation. For digital government to succeed in the future, it's critical to ensure that such systems don't place unreasonable demands on the people they're designed to protect.

A major challenge for any kind of big-data software deployment is that, based on simple statistics, tiny data problems end up hurting a lot of people. That's why processes need to be significantly improved first, and only then automated to run faster. As automated services get connected and become reliant on one other, simple oversights in one database might end up creating problems in many other systems, as the next story shows.

THE GRAND RAPIDS MASSACRE

The days between Christmas and New Year's Day are, for most people on the planet, a period of joy and celebration. For medical emergency services, though, this is one of the busiest times of the year. Partying too hard mostly leads to bad hangovers, but the period also marks a sharp increase in accidents and fatalities. Still, the sheer scale of deaths in Grand Rapids, USA, in 2003 surprised everyone. During the Christmas holidays that year, more than 8500 people were declared dead in the St Mary's Mercy Medical Center, in an unexplained epidemic that cost the city of Grand Rapids almost 5% of its population. One of the casualties was Cathy Uhl, a 55-year-old administrative supervisor at the Grand Rapids Press. When the postman delivered Uhl's final medical bill on 2 January, she was quite shocked to learn that she had, in fact, been dead for a while.

After a 'routine' upgrade of the record management system at the hospital, the computers dropped one digit from the code indicating that a patient had been discharged home. Instead, everyone who'd visited the hospital between October and December the previous year was marked as deceased. Jennifer Cammenga, a spokesperson for the hospital, attributed the problem to a simple mapping error, but it's questionable whether she could be trusted. After all, according to hospital records, Cammenga was among the walking dead.

The computer glitch didn't just stop at sending wrong medical bills. By virtue of everything being connected to everything else these days, the hospital systems also directly notified computers at several other organisations, including the government. Connected medical insurance companies started taking people off their registers. Roughly 2800 Medicare accounts were at risk, because insurers might have refused to cover additional bills after a person had (wrongly) been given a date of death.

Software teams often test upgrades on a small idealistic data sample. But the real world is messy, inconsistent and full of weird cases that fall outside the norm. That's why a routine upgrade can mess up important information or remove it by mistake. Problems with legacy data get even worse when software is replaced rather than upgraded. Years of undocumented glitches and workarounds embedded in the old system get thrown away. However, the old data sticks around, and the new system often isn't ready to deal with all the peculiarities.

When the Blue Cross insurance company in North Carolina moved 500,000 customers from a 15-year-old system to new software in January 2016, its call centre was overwhelmed by confused clients. Among the people participating in the 500% increase in call volume were Jim and Kathy Kluth. They'd switched to a joint insurance plan a month before the data upgrade. The Kluths received three different insurance ID numbers. Blue Cross incorrectly debited both the new and the old plan premium from their bank account, requiring Jim and Kathy to spend 12 hours on the phone with the insurer to get the money back. Beth Anne Corriveau received an insurance policy covering the year 2199. The system insisted that Beth's account was actually delinquent, as her credit apparently expired in 1753. The Charlotte Observer reported that some customers had been accidentally dropped from the system, and that some had received insurance ID cards with invalid numbers. Roughly 25,000 customers were assigned to a wrong healthcare plan, leading to wrong account charges.

The Blue Cross chaos was actually part of a staged roll-out of a new system, with the insurance company explaining to the press that some glitches are expected when upgrading complex IT systems. From a management perspective, it's easy to look at the statistics and declare that something that worked 95% of the time was a relative success. But I bet that the thousands of people who got caught by the bugs weren't too happy to just be rounding errors.

In most data upgrade scenarios, the freak cases become clear pretty quickly, and administrative staff then have to deal with a few weeks of chaos until the new software settles in. From a management perspective, a few weeks of adjustments might sound like an acceptable trade-off for a system that will run for years, but even a few weeks is long enough to cause serious damage.

For example, Dallas police replaced a 30-year-old case management system in 2014, aiming to store all related case records in a single place. Two weeks later, the software caused more than 20 people to be released from prison without posting any bail. The new system was less forgiving than the old one, and case workers had to fix many old reports that were originally entered with mistakes. One of the expected benefits of the new system was speeding up communication with prosecutors. Ironically, the backlog of fixing work built up so much that officers didn't have time to promptly deal with incoming cases, so many newly arrested people had to be released. Two men who walked out without bail committed a violent robbery just three days later.

Migrating data from one system to another is always risky, because years of unofficial workarounds, hidden assumptions and unsolved problems will come to light. The St Mary's hospital upgrade shows the dangers of a new system doing something unexpected, but at least in such cases the problems are easy to spot. When the new system stops doing something it should, the problems are a lot more difficult to detect, so they can stay under the radar for a long time. That's the topic of the next story.

POLICE E-MAIL

In 2005, in California, USA, 17 counties rolled out CalWIN, a new system for managing Medicare insurance. CalWIN is short for CalWORKs Information Network, which in turn is short for California Work Opportunity and Responsibility to Kids. With such a complicated name, it was almost expected that the new system would have some serious teething problems. A few months after the roll-out, some clients started noticing problems with their medical bills. In March 2006, Juan Ledezma received a $786 bill that should have been covered by Medicare, and then discovered that he was no longer in the system. Unlike the old software, CalWIN mistakenly removed eligible recipients unless they logged on to explicitly extend cover.

One of the most common wrong assumptions software developers make about the world is that everyone is connected to the Internet as well as they are, and has access to the same types of modern gadgets. That's why many modern systems put the burden for missing out on important notifications on the recipients, not the sender.

Christopher McMahon, living in Cape Coral in Florida, discovered this first hand in February 2014. Standing in a checkout line with a bag full of groceries, he swiped his benefits card, but there was no money on it. Back then, McMahon received help from the Supplemental Nutrition Assistance Program (SNAP). SNAP provides temporary financial support for low-income families, and participants need to certify their eligibility every six months. McMahon's case had been up for review in January, but due to a software glitch in the notification system, McMahon never got the memo. And he was not alone. Some 27,000 people out of 200,000 scheduled for review didn't get the reminder in January. The SNAP glitch returned two years later, doubling the effects. In September 2016, around 48,000 people were mistakenly removed from the notification list. As a result, 25,000 eligible families failed to report back on time.

It's almost impossible for people to know that they're missing out on important information if they weren't expecting it in the first place. But with such an overflow of digital communication these days, even people who expect to be notified might not notice when something important gets lost in transit.

In January 2015, the Queensland Department of Education in Australia upgraded its OneSchool software for students' personal information. The change was supposed to improve the mandatory child protection reports, sending the most critical messages directly to the Queensland Police Service. Seven months later, developers investigating an unrelated problem discovered more than 1000 messages that had never made it out of the system, although they were marked as successfully sent. All those notifications were intended for the police only, with reports of serious abuse. The glitch caused a crisis in the Department of Education, and the deputy director-general for state schools called it 'the most serious situation we had ever faced at head office'. The minister for education hired an external auditor to determine the cause of the problem, and it all came down to a simple coding bug. To prevent spam and e-mail abuse, the system automatically blocked e-mails that were not directly addressed to an e-mail address from the communities.qld.gov.au domain. Messages intended only for the police were sent to a different domain, and just went into a black hole.

Unfortunately, this wasn't an isolated incident. The Florida Abuse Hotline suffered a similar glitch in 2017. The Hotline is the primary contact centre for reporting child abuse in Florida, USA. Call centre staff usually note down basic information before transferring a call to a case worker; in cases when the call drops before being transferred, this critical information would go directly to the police. After a software upgrade on 4 February, this information was no longer sent, and nobody noticed it for more than two months.

Unfortunately, with such reliance on a myriad of different systems to complete work, it's not enough to just schedule a notification and blindly trust that it will be delivered. The Florida Department of Children and Families decided to implement a separate monitoring system to check whether delivery backlogs were building up, which was definitely a step in the right direction. In fact, most problems with unattended automation mentioned in this part of the book would have been solved if only someone had been paying attention to obvious signs of trouble.

GIRLS, ALCOHOL, COCAINE AND WHATEVER

In a major initiative to reduce tobacco addiction, governments around the world started to ban smoking in public places at the turn of the century. To further cement the idea that smoking is not some cheap form of stress-relief but an expensive, unhealthy addiction, taxes on tobacco were also increased. The reasoning was simple: when prices surge, sales will plummet. For Josh Muszynski from New Hampshire, USA, the straw that broke the camel's back was actually a pack of Camel cigarettes. Or, more accurately, a pack of Camel broke his bank account. After Josh picked up his favourite smokes in 2009 from a local petrol station, Bank of America fined him $15 dollars for spending over his account limit. Convinced that this was an error, Muszynski phoned his bank to complain, only to be told that the cigarettes had cost him $23,148,855,308,184,500. For the scientifically inclined, this is 23 quadrillion dollars, and some change. No wonder Bank of America was asking for a $15 transaction fee. After two hours on the phone with various banking departments, Josh was able to convince the masters of finance that 2000 times the cost of the US national debt was not a reasonable price for a pack of Camel, regardless of taxes.

Most money today moves without any human involvement. This saves time and makes transactions cheaper, but it also means that careless mistakes become more difficult to spot. And when banking computers make mistakes, it's the consumers who are often on the hook to prove their innocence. Muszynski was lucky that the charge on his account was so outrageous it was clearly an error. The mistake may have been less easy to resolve if the amount had been only a few dollars. The cause was, according to a CNN report, a 'temporary programming error at Visa Debit Processing Services'. But temporary, when the whole processing chain is made of computers, doesn't necessarily mean small. A representative of Visa said the error had affected almost 13,000 transactions.

Money movements were automated decades ago, but the trend of automation continues, along with all its blind spots. Software-enabled service companies can easily undercut their competitors, so people are promptly disappearing from many customer-service processes. When I wrote this in 2017, the new global software taxi companies were the prime example of this trend. By fully automating booking, dispatching and coordinating drivers and pricing the rides, Uber and its clones can transport customers more conveniently and cheaply than traditional taxi cabs. (If you're reading this a few years after the book was published, I wouldn't be surprised if people had been removed altogether from driving.) When computers are doing so much without any oversight, it's not easy to spot mistakes. One Uber customer in Philadelphia went for a short city ride in 2016, at the amazing cost of $28,639.14. She hopped in and out around the city, and error-prone computers agreed among themselves how much to bill, without anyone even considering whether it would have been cheaper to get a first class airline ticket around the world, airport transfers included. The passenger only noticed the problem after the bank blocked her card.

Of course, computers aren't biased, so they can happily make mistakes against both sides in a transaction. Paul Fischer, CFO of Windsor Group in Florida, moved some money between two of his company accounts on 26 March 2010. Money transfers between accounts are one of the least exciting things you can do on a Friday evening. At the end, the total tends to always be the same. That Friday, however, the SunTrust bank added a thank-you tip for a loyal customer, topping up the balance to exactly $88,888,888,888.88. Fisher decided to play fair and called the bank to report the problem, and by Saturday morning all the money was gone.

For an evening, Windsor Group was one of the world's most valuable companies, but the extent of its short-lived good fortune is hardly a record setter. That honour belongs to Chris Reynolds from Pennsylvania, a recipient of PayPal's most generous bug ever. For a few hours in 2013, his account showed a balance of more than $92 quadrillion dollars. Just to put that into perspective, it was a million times more than the estimated net worth of the richest person alive. Or, from a different perspective, enough for four whole packs of Muszynski's Camels.

The nice thing about electronic money is that it can be moved much more easily than physical cash. For example, when Jeff Ferrera called the First National Bank of Chicago to check his balance in 1996, both he and the clerk at the other end of the telephone line were surprised by a payment of $924,844,208.32. In gold, this would weigh roughly 50 metric tonnes, so there would be no way for someone like Jeff to carry it himself. But the bad thing about electronic money is that, unlike gold, computers can also invent it out of thin air. Jeff wasn't the only new almost-billionaire that day. In total, the First National Bank magicked up $763.8 billion, almost 10% of the GDP of the USA that year, and deposited it into several customer accounts.

When a computer bug breaks the bank, it's easy to find people screaming. But when the mistakes are small, the problems can stay under the radar for a long time. Luke Moore from Goulburn, in Australia, made the news in 2016 after a judge ruled that 'a human could not be found guilty of deceiving a computer'. Six years earlier, Moore had lost his job and been involved in a bad car accident. Soon, he no longer had enough money to make the mortgage payments. Moore was expecting to get kicked out of his house any day, but the AU$500 instalment just went through. So did the next one. And the one after that. After a whole year had passed, Moore's bank was still making payments every fortnight. For some reason, although Moore was unemployed and living on welfare benefits, St George Bank gave him a huge credit limit. Moore decided to test just how huge. He called the home loan company instructing it to draw AU$5000 immediately. That went through, so he called the company a few days later asking to draw AU$50,000. The computers didn't complain. Soon after, Moore was behind the wheel of a brand new Alfa Romeo 156. Then he bought a glass-roof Hyundai Veloster, just so he could drive 120 miles to Sydney to buy a Maserati.

Encouraged by the endless line of credit, Moore moved to the Gold Coast, and of course bought a fishing boat. According to his own account, he spent 'hundreds of thousands of dollars on girls, alcohol, cocaine and whatever'. By the time the St George

Bank figured out what was going on, it had already loaned AU\$1,988,535.25 to Moore. Moore was arrested in December 2012. Because he was suddenly broke again, Moore couldn't even afford to hire lawyers, so he had to get help through legal aid. The Sydney District Court found Moore guilty of obtaining financial benefit by deception in 2015, and sentenced him to four and a half years in prison. Disappointed with his defence lawyers, Moore started to read legal books while serving the sentence. Six months later, he found a loophole that got him a retrial, bail, and ultimately freedom. He was able to prove that he had 'no legal obligation to inform the bank of what was going on', so though the bank lost money, that's because its computers were too permissive with credits, and there was no crime. When I wrote this, Moore was free and busy studying law.

Moore's story, although fascinating, isn't the only such case, or even the worst. In 2012, something oddly similar happened to Christine Lee, an engineering student who lived in Sydney. Computers at Westpac, a major Australian bank, for some reason decided to give her unlimited credit. This was despite the fact that she was only 17 years old at the time, and in Australia on a student visa. On 22 July, when a monthly rent payment put the account into overdraft, Lee noticed that something wasn't exactly right. After a few more payments went through, Lee started buying luxury goods and transferring money into other accounts. Four years later, she was arrested at an airport trying to flee the police. The bank managed to recover AU\$1.3 million that Lee had moved to other accounts, but not more than AU\$3.3 million of the amount she had spent on handbags, clothes, jewellery and shoes. Lee was charged for the same crime as Luke Moore. When I wrote this, her case was still going through courts, so the story was far from over.

All these cases illustrate an undeniable truth. Unattended automation of money makes it difficult to spot mistakes. That's why it's so important to build in early warning systems and monitor outliers, so that people at least discover problems quickly.

WILD, WILD TECH

Modern computers may be able to stream your favourite political satire, show photos in millions of vibrant colours and play songs to draw tears, but they're cold machines that don't understand or care too much for any of that. Even the funniest cat videos on YouTube are nothing more than 1s and 0s to our digital companions. It's up to humans to interpret all that information, and many stupid problems are born in the gap between human perception and computer reality.

The stories in this part explore the surprises caused by modern technology and its limitations.

THE NORTHUMBRIAN COFFEE PARTY

As the personal information for new admissions started flowing into the school systems in the USA in 2014, many college administrators noticed an interesting trend. Significantly more rich kids were signing up to attend school than in previous years. Thousands of teenagers with salaries worthy of Fortune 500 CEOs suddenly decided to enrol into colleges, especially in the poorer areas. Of course, the US economy didn't suddenly boom overnight. This was all caused by a software bug misplacing a simple point.

Some parts of the Institutional Student Information Records (ISIRs) came from the Federal Student Aid agency, which allocates more than $120 billion yearly in financial aid to college and university students, mostly from low-income families. In order to decide who gets how much money, the agency requires applicants to provide extensive background information on their education, family situation and recent sources of income. The FAFSA form, short for the Free Application for Federal Student Aid, is a daunting piece of bureaucracy. It contains more than 100 questions spread over five pages, with five more pages just for instructions.

Hoping to speed up the application process and make it less error prone, the authorities introduced a new online version of the form in 2014. Instead of students being expected to read detailed instructions, the software could help them fill the form in correctly. While it's easy for people to understand that 1000, 1,000 and $1,000 refer to the same amount, computers need a single, standardised format to compare all the applications. So the forms-processing software automatically corrected small inconsistencies, for example by discarding dollar signs and commas. But it went too far and also discarded decimal points.

Roughly 200,000 meticulous students entered their income with cents. Instead of rounding the amounts, or even reporting an error, the application-processing software accepted the numbers, but just the digits. This meant that a student earning $5000 would incorrectly be labelled as someone who made half a million, significantly reducing the student's chance of getting any federal grants. The wrong numbers completely mixed up grant allocations. Some ineligible students were selected for aid; some people didn't qualify, despite their low income. Even when the software correctly approved a grant, because of the wrong data about the other students, the amounts might have been incorrect. Once school administrators started noticing the wrong information, the agency had to recalculate the whole grant allocation for the year and update all the student records.

It seems silly for a single decimal point to cause so much trouble, but mistakes with decimals are one of the most common, and most costly, software blunders. Decimal point problems are mostly caused by bad user interfaces that fail to communicate expectations or validate user input. But the problems are rarely noticed there. Instead, the bad data propagates through other systems, which blindly trust the original information, until a person needs to look at it.

In 2013, Stephanie Banks took a $300 loan from Rapid Cash in south-east Portland, USA. Two years later, she got a letter from a third-party debt collection agency, asking for a prompt payment of $40,317. After journalists from OregonLive.com picked up the story, a Rapid Cash manager admitted the mistake. The loan payment request should have been for $403.17, and the decimals somehow got mixed up.

Of course, you don't need a person to input the wrong numbers for decimal mistakes; computers can do that themselves, and at scale. Betty Williams of Columbus, Indiana, USA, checked out of a local Holiday Inn in October 2002 with a receipt for $176, but her credit card was charged a hefty $17,600. She discovered the error while trying to pay for food at a local grocery store, when her card was declined. And she wasn't alone. Some 26,000 people who stayed at Holiday Inn, Holiday Inn Express or Crowne Plaza in the last week of October that year ended up with surprising bills. The hotels blamed their credit processor, First Horizon Merchant, for messing up the decimal points on payments.

Decimal issues with unattended electronic payment systems can easily leave people without money for basic needs. Laura Newman from Prestbury, UK, had to borrow money to buy food for her family when her bank account went into overdraft in April 2016. At the start of the month, she took a rental car from Hertz. Instead of £340 for the three day rental, Hertz charged Newman £34,000. More surprisingly, Newman's bank let the transaction go through, even though there wasn't enough money in the account, pushing her into debit. The problem was resolved once Mirror journalists reported on the story.

Jonathan Mortimer suffered a similar fate to Laura Newman after cancelling his mobile phone contract with O2 in Worcester, UK, in February 2016. Due to an early contract cancellation, Mortimer had to pay a £17.64 fee, but O2 took £1,764 from his account. According to a report in the Mirror, Mortimer had to borrow money from relatives to pay his mortgage while the bank and the mobile provider argued who was to blame.

Just to prove that computers aren't biased against people, Amsterdam surprised almost 10,000 of its poor residents with an interesting Christmas gift in late 2013. Dutch news site AT5 published a picture of the bank statement for one lucky citizen, who received €15,500 in benefits instead of the usual €155. In a fantastic case of a displaced decimal point, the city ended up paying €188 million for housing assistance instead of €1.88 million. During the course of the next few months, the city was able to recover almost all the overpaid money. The final bill came to about €2.4 million in unrecoverable payments, and more than €300,000 spent managing the whole blunder.

Misplaced decimals don't even need to be about money to cause trouble. Denise Garrido from Bradford, Ontario, Canada, knows that best. Garrido won the Miss Universe Canada title in May 2013, only to lose it the next day. An employee of the Miss Universe organiser missed a decimal point when typing up the judges' votes, and the computer declared a wrong winner. After the error was fixed, Garrido dropped to fourth place.

The biggest decimal blunder, however, has to be that in the experiment conducted at Northumbria University, Newcastle, UK, in March 2015. The goal of the research was to measure the effects of caffeine on sport. Alex Rossetta and Luke Parkin, students at the university, volunteered to perform exercises while taking various doses of caffeine. In order to get precise results, university researchers gave students caffeine in powder form, measured to a tenth of a gram. Unfortunately, they calculated the weight with the help of their mobile phones, and with a decimal point in the wrong place. Instead of the equivalent of three cups of coffee, Rossetta and Parkin each consumed something close to three hundred espressos. They quickly collapsed, experienced violent side-effects, and had to be rushed to the hospital intensive care unit. Both men eventually recovered, though Rossetta suffered from short-term memory loss. Newcastle Crown Court later fined the university £400,000 over the blunder.

One way to avoid decimal point mistakes is to require users to always enter information consistently, for example for amounts to always come with two decimals. Unfortunately, that's not enough to lift the decimal curse. Even if all the points are in the right place, computers can mess up badly when processing lots of numbers. That's the topic of the next story.

ROUNDING UP
THE PARLIAMENT

One of the most common marketing clichés is that there's no such thing as bad publicity. The owners of the T4 Cafe in Fremont, California, USA, would likely disagree. Their shop ended up on national television in April 2017, with claims that they were overcharging customers. NBC TV followed up on the lead from Mary Lai, a local resident, who noticed that she was paying too much sales tax for her milkshakes. Lai noticed that the tax on small purchases often got rounded up to a cent. Rounding errors are a common cause of small and insignificant mistakes; this rounding error might have been small, but it was far from insignificant. NBC journalists got in touch with Venus Stromberg from the State Board of Equalization, the government body that controls sales taxes in California, who confirmed that the amounts were wrong and warned that such miscalculations could count as serious tax fraud.

Although modern computers can handle numbers with mind-boggling precision, financial amounts for most everyday purposes are rounded to the smallest currency. For the USA, that means one cent. Multiplying small amounts with tax percentages often produces numbers that have fractions of cents, so someone has to win or lose a tiny amount on each such transaction. Contrary to the basic arithmetic taught in schools, rounding financial amounts is far from a trivial task, riddled with politics and arbitrary rules, and it's very easy to get it wrong. That's why each tax authority has its own system for rounding the tax.

Using a trivial rounding system for money isn't just a legal issue, it might end up effectively printing money. For example, at the introduction of the euro currency, the rate of German marks to euro was fixed at 1.94 to 1. By using the usual school arithmetic, 0.01 euro would equal 0.02 marks (0.00515 rounded to two decimals). At the same time, 0.01 marks would equal 0.01 euro (0.0194 rounded to two decimals). It was theoretically possible to convert a single euro-cent into two pfennigs, but then convert each of those two pfennigs back into two euro-cents separately, effectively magicking a cent from thin air. At the time when I wrote this in 2017, the Google Search foreign exchange calculator still fell for that trick (type 'euro to dm exchange rate' into Google Search to play with it). That's why the introduction of the Euro came with strict rounding and conversion rules.

Unless you've worked in financial markets, legally regulating cent rounding might sound silly, but consider this example. I used to work with a UK company that integrated with a global online poker network. The poker network mostly targeted US customers, so the value of a poker chip was 1 dollar cent. The UK company held money in British pounds, so its customers had to buy and sell chips in order to play poker. The developers building the screen for chip purchases didn't understand that they were effectively doing foreign exchange, but one of the customers knew exactly what was going on. Back in 2005, when the dollar to pound exchange rate was roughly 0.54, the customer exchanged £0.01 for two poker chips (0.0185 rounded to two decimals), then exchanged each of those chips back into £0.01 (0.0054 rounded to two decimals). With some basic web browser automation, the savvy user generated more than £10,000 overnight and then transferred the money to his bank account. Because the customer just used the system as designed, the company had to pay it out.

Although financial institutions take maths more seriously than the average person does, that doesn't mean they're immune to computer rounding problems. Way back in January 1981, the Vancouver Stock Exchange launched a new stock price index. A stock market index is a rough but quick way to show the overall performance of the market, and such numbers are often used by the media to show investment trends, and even as an indicator of the strength of the national economy. The Vancouver index started at 1000 points, and by November 1983 had lost almost half its value, falling to 524.811. The Canadian economy wasn't going bankrupt, though; someone discovered that the index had incorrectly rounded individual transactions. After a recalculation, the index resumed at 1098.892, almost twice the value.

Tiny rounding errors can easily stay undetected for a long time and continue growing into a serious amount of cash. The most costly case of rounding errors is likely to be AXA Rosenberg's risk Optimizer. The Optimizer software incorrectly combined information from several risk models, some in decimals and some specified as percentages. Over time, this error caused over $216 million in losses for 608 out of 1421 client portfolios managed by the AXA Rosenberg Group. The Securities and Exchange Commission charged AXA Rosenberg with securities fraud, leading to a settlement in 2011 costing more than $240 million in fines and refunds.

Tax and foreign exchange are highly regulated, but the calculations that don't directly affect government income are far less likely to have strict rules attached. Software developers automating the rounding for non-financial quantities can make their own assumptions about what's fair. Unfortunately, small errors can add up to a big mess when done on large scale.

For example, in April 2017, citizens of Shreveport in Louisiana, USA, took the local city council to court for rounding errors on gallons for their water utility bills. In the UK, the telecoms regulator, Ofcom, opened an investigation into British Telecom's billing practices in 2013, after claims that it was overcharging customers by rounding the time spent on calls. The same year, the UK Office of Gas and Electricity Markets raised concerns that several energy utility companies were overcharging customers by rounding gas calories to different numbers of decimals. EON had to return £2.5 million to consumers. With the others, the situation wasn't so clear cut. After arguments about different rounding policies, instead of paying fines or refunding consumers, EDF Energy and British Gas ended up donating millions of pounds to trust funds for helping vulnerable customers.

Utility bills translate some other type of resource to money, so it's easy to spot and argue about potential rounding problems. But computer rounding can still have an impact on people on a large scale, even if it doesn't relate to money. Way back in 1992, this was perfectly demonstrated by the local elections in Germany. On 5 April 1992, in the German state of Schleswig-Holstein, the elections did not result in a clear majority for any party. The single elected representative of the Green party had the power to play the king-maker, with 5% of the electoral votes. At the time, election rules required parties to pass a 5% threshold to get a seat in the parliament. After the results were published, with so much at stake, someone recalculated the numbers and discovered that the Greens actually had just 4.97% of the votes. The election counting software, which had been used for years, rounded up the numbers. By removing the Green party from the seat allocation, the Social Democrats achieved a single-person majority in the Schleswig-Holstein parliament, easily forming a stable government.

Decimal rounding is such a wonderful bug magnet, because it's intuitively clear to everyone, but actual usage for different business purposes often requires following specialist rules, expert domain knowledge, and doing things counter-intuitively.

Numbers are, in fact, the simplest type of data for computers. All that computers know is numbers anyway. Other types of information, such as text or dates, need to be translated into numbers first so computers can understand them. This opens up plenty of opportunities for erroneous assumptions and avoidable bugs, as the next few stories show.

UNICODE
OF DEATH

Smartphones brought us mobile Internet, thousands of songs in our pockets, and a million auto-correct errors and apologies for fat-finger typing. For the younger generations, the mobile phone revolution reversed thousands of years of civilisation, at least when it comes to literacy. Instead of writing with symbols that represent sounds, teenagers today communicate using emojis, modern versions of ancient pictograms. Similar to hieroglyphs, the symbols alone are not enough to understand an emoji message. Sequence, size and different ways of combining pictures all have a meaning. Clock, pig face, airplane means 'when pigs fly'. Gun, money bag, car means 'let's rob a bank'. Receiving a message with a white flag, zero and rainbow – well, if you had an iPhone or iPad in January 2017, it likely meant that your phone was about to freeze.

The white-flag iPhone prank first appeared on YouTube on 17 January 2017 and quickly became viral. Just receiving the specially crafted message would cause phones to immediately become unresponsive and, after a while, crash. The trick worked in direct messages, group chats, even with sharing contact cards. The problem affected iPads as well, and even some MacBook computers. There was pretty much nothing the target of the prank could do to prevent the crash. For some strange reason, iPhones found special meaning in the sequence of those emojis, and decided it was time to panic.

Ever since computers could print out information, people have found a way to taunt them with specially crafted messages. In high school, back at the time of the ancient DOS systems and Novell Netware networks, we confused teachers by sending them messages containing the ASCII 7 character – aptly named BELL – which would make their computers beep.

With ubiquitous connectivity, the modern equivalents of such pranks can now run at a massive scale. And with messages stored in computing clouds, they can keep coming back indefinitely. In June 2015, a nasty bug in Skype appeared. Messages containing the text http://: would crash Skype on Windows, Android and iOS. Restarting the application wouldn't help much, because Skype would try to redisplay the recent messages, and crash. Re-installing the application didn't help either, because Skype would try to download the recent history from the Internet automatically, and commit suicide again.

The problem was simple, and to Skype's credit, it was fixed in less than a day. Instead of just displaying messages, Skype processes hyperlinks from the messages to display thumbnails and link to remote resources. The text http://: starts like a typical hyperlink but only has a colon instead of the remote address. Most likely, Skype only checked whether a piece of text started like a hyperlink to decide whether to apply special processing, and crashed because the rest of the link wasn't valid.

The iPhone emoji bug with the white flag was caused by something very similar – an invalid emoji variation. Although sending smileys with top-hats today seems quite easy, enabling a diverse set of devices such as phones, computers and even refrigerator screens to display such messages correctly is quite a technological feat. Computers only deal with numbers; they don't really have a notion of text. Unicode is a global agreement on how to use numbers to represent most of the letters and symbols used by various written languages around the world. It helps pretty much all modern technology to display text on a screen correctly, regardless of where that text was composed. In addition to letters and writing symbols, Unicode specifies how to represent common special characters, such as lines, arrows and hearts. As mobile phones took off and teenagers rejected letters in favour of pictograms, Unicode expanded to include hundreds of emojis as well. In order to capture so many different symbols with a limited set of numbers, Unicode includes special processing codes that control how the text should be displayed. These special codes specify the direction of writing and how to combine or modify other symbols. That's where the fun really starts, because such codes turn simple text into a set of commands for the computer to execute, which always opens the door to bugs.

Similar to the Skype invalid hyperlink, invalid control sequences can send the software that tries to interpret Unicode text into a state of shock. In the case of the white-flag message, the culprit was a variation selector. In order to avoid creating a separate code for each colour variant of each emoji, Unicode allows mixing basic symbols with colours using a variation selector. A white flag, variation selector and rainbow would normally produce a rainbow-coloured flag. To people, variation selectors are invisible, but computers recognise what they need to do. The flag prank message put a zero between the variation selector and the rainbow, making the whole sequence invalid. But the iOS Unicode handling software didn't check for valid sequences correctly, tried to find a resulting emoji, then gave up in despair. It's a weird bug, but hardly an unpredictable one.

In fact, similar bugs happen every few years. In 2015, a combination of Arabic, Marathi and Chinese letters got in the news because it could cause iPhones to restart remotely. If a phone is locked when it receives an SMS message, it normally tries to abbreviate it to fit in a few lines then display on the lock screen. Unfortunately, abbreviating a message with such a mix of languages triggered a bug in the text display module, and the phones would immediately crash.

The most famous Unicode display bug was discovered by Russian software developer Pavel Zhovner in 2013. Putting a piece of text including some garbled Arabic characters into a web page, Zhovner found out that he could crash the Safari browser on Mac computers and iOS devices. The Chrome browser on Mac computers was also affected, but less drastically – it would just refuse to display web pages containing that text. SMS messages containing the garbled Arabic text would cause the Messages application on iPhones to crash, and it would keep crashing if users tried to restart it. The Apple Messages application for Mac computers would also run away in panic. The error, it turned out, was deep in Apple's CoreText text-processing system, so people kept discovering new ways of misusing it. For example, putting the text into the name of a Wi-Fi network could cause nearby phones to crash if they tried to show a list of available connections. Because of the widespread impact, the text message became known as the Unicode of Death.

Although all the examples here are from messaging applications, Unicode display bugs affect other software, too. Messaging is just a way to spread the problem quickly. Any application that converts text into some other format, such as exporting a document to an image, needs to be able to deal with potential Unicode land-mines. In order to cover every imaginable writing need, Unicode is today so complex that it's very easy to make silly oversights. To add insult to injury, as of 2017, it was still rapidly evolving as a standard, so it's likely to introduce new loopholes in the future.

Yet you don't have to look for the insane complexity of handling all possible written languages ever in order to find problems with translating the real world into digital records. Something as simple as a calendar is enough to cause trouble, as you'll see in the next story.

THAT '70s IPHONE

Apple products are famous for hidden references to pop culture, computer history and inside jokes. After the release of the Lego Batman Movie, the digital assistant Siri could turn an iPhone into the Bat-computer if you knew the magic words. iOS 8.3 allowed Star Trek fans to unlock a special Vulcan salute emoji. When some versions of the OS X operating system download files, incomplete items show 24 January 1984 as the creation date – the moment when Steve Jobs introduced the original Macintosh computer.

Apple fans love these virtual Easter eggs, and discovering a new one always makes a big splash in social media. On Valentine's Day 2016, a new trick spread through message boards to unlock a retro visual look for iPhones. The suggestion was: set the date back to 1 January 1970, restart the device, and you'll see a '70s Macintosh boot-up process, complete with the famous rainbow icon. But, instead of an Easter egg, the process triggered a dangerous bug.

Anyone who's ever seen a sci-fi movie knows that time travel is dangerous if you go too far into the past. And January 1970 is too far for an iPhone. There was no '70s Macintosh boot-up process, as the Mac was first introduced in 1984. Even worse, the Apple Computer company was only founded in 1976. Phones set to 1970 would get stuck during the start-up process, and there was pretty much nothing helpless users could do on their own to repair the situation. The broken phones had to be taken to a shop for replacement.

The cause of the iPhone issue was never officially confirmed, but 1 January 1970 is a special date for computing, and often linked to two common sources of wrong assumptions. Although people might like to think about dates, computers only store information as numbers. A large majority of computing devices record time as seconds since the start of 1970 in Coordinated Universal Time (UTC). That makes 1 January 1970 effectively day zero for most phones, computers, digital watches or even home appliances. That's why so many people complain online that their microwave time-travelled to the '70s after a power cut.

The first potential problem with that date is that the number zero is sometimes used to signal an invalid or missing value, especially for numeric data fields, so some system library might explode on receiving a 'missing' date. By setting the date to 1 January, people in time zones east of Greenwich might actually be setting their internal clock to negative time. The second potential cause of problems is that developers expect time to always be a positive number.

Security researchers Patrick Kelley and Matt Harrigan took the Zero-Date problem to a completely new level. The original Valentine's Day hoax got owners to set the date on their devices manually, but Kelley and Harrigan wanted to automate the whole process. With just $120 worth of equipment, they were able to remotely trick iOS devices to self-destruct.

Most portable Apple devices automatically connect to previously known Wi-Fi networks. Anyone can easily set up a fake open wireless network under a common name, for example the name used by a popular hotel or a coffee shop chain, and trick nearby iOS gadgets to connect. On its own, this is a minor security risk but nothing too serious. By controlling the wireless network, however, the security researchers could spoof the address of time. apple.com to provide fake time information, and devices would automatically update their internal clocks. Time travel got most test phones and tablets to start misbehaving, crash and restart on their own. Most devices started to heat up as applications continuously crashed and competed for resources. Several iPads started counting time backwards, reaching well into 1965. One tablet reached 54 degrees Celsius (130 Fahrenheit) before finally committing suicide.

Apple finally plugged the retro iPhone bricking loophole with iOS 9.3, on 21 March 2016, but iPhone users then started reporting that they received phantom e-mails from 1970. Apart from the strange fact that e-mail was not invented until 1972, those messages were empty, without a subject or a body, and could not be deleted.

The combination of storing dates as numbers and marking missing or incomplete information with special numbers such as 0 or −1 pretty much guarantees that seeing 1 January 1970 means there's a bug somewhere. For people living in the USA, or in fact anywhere west of the Greenwich time zone, 31 December 1969 plays the same role.

Apple is not alone in having problems with date zero. PayPal had a glitch in June 2016 showing that some accounts were frozen until 31 December 1969. On New Year's Day in 2016, some Facebook users got congratulations for being friends with someone else on the site for 46 years, despite the fact that Facebook launched in the mid-2000s and that most of its users are younger than 46. Do the maths quickly and find the date exactly 46 years before New Year in 2016.

Another common problem with dates is the upper limit. Unlike real calendars, that will go on forever, digital calendars have to end somewhere. We explore that problem in the next story.

FEBRUARY 2038

Scandinavian countries are known for their great government services. The Central School in Tierp, a town in Sweden with 5507 residents, worked with the population registry in 2012 to ensure that all eligible preschool children were notified about the start of a new school year. In Sweden, education is compulsory. Anna was born in '07, just like all the other children on the list, but couldn't come to school. Instead of Anna's parents, it was her daughter who responded to the letter from the school. Ms Eriksson was indeed born in '07, but it was the wrong century. At 105, she was just a bit too old for school.

Long time periods tend to cause problems with computers, as software is rarely designed with longevity in mind. Most modern devices keep time by measuring the number of seconds since 1 January 1970, the so-called Unix epoch. On 29 January 2038, around 3am GMT, Unix epoch timestamps will go over the storage limit for 32-bit signed integers. Due to how integer arithmetic works on computers, 32-bit dates will go into negative values at that point. Comparing numbers, the timestamp for 31 January 2038 will be before the timestamp for 28 January the same year or even the timestamp for when I wrote this in 2017. Software developers rarely consider the possibility of non-continuous time – that sounds like something that belongs more to a Tarantino film than computer software.

Timestamp overflows end up hurting organisations with much higher budgets and more serious software developers than Scandinavian schools have. For example, the US Congressional Budget Office (CBO) unsuccessfully tried to run its long-term forecasting models in 2011. Whenever the CBO tried to estimate spending over more than 30 years, its software crashed. According to a CNS News report, congressman Paul Ryan interpreted that as a comment on the current government policies, saying that 'The CBO can't conceive of any way in which the economy can continue past the year 2037.' The reality is, unfortunately, a lot less dramatic: running a 30-year model starting in 2011 puts the period over the year 2038.

Problems with timestamp overflows aren't a particularly new phenomenon. PDP-10 computers used 12-bit integers for dates and ended up crashing horribly when that limit was exhausted way back in 1975. In theory, we should know how to deal with timestamp limits by now. Yet in August 2013, NASA lost contact with its Deep Impact space probe after the onboard computers started continuously rebooting themselves. Deep Impact had tracked time with one-tenths of a second since the start of year 2000, and stopped talking to mission control the day those time-stamps went over the limit of 32-bit integers.

The lovely thing about year 2038 is that everything should work OK, as far as the computing architecture is concerned. The problem was discovered and addressed well ahead of time. Most modern devices and applications execute on 64-bit hardware and operating systems, which have much larger storage limits. Still, Internet discussion boards are full of complaints that MYSQL, a popular database, has weird bugs with dates after the year 2038. The fact remains that, even today, 32-bit timestamps are quite popular for storage systems where size efficiency is critical, for example recording a huge number of transactions, or exports to file formats optimised for size. This makes it possible to play some intriguing arbitrage between different layers of complex software applications.

You might be able to enter a date in the user interface that the back-end cannot record properly. The scope for strange effects wasn't lost on the enterprising players of freemium games, who discovered that by setting the date beyond 2038 on their Android devices they could time-travel into the past. Freemium games often extract money by making players wait unless they pay. But few developers expected time to start flowing in the opposite direction, which made for some quite exciting hacks.

Apple devices, ever more locked down than Android, prevent the date trick at the operating system level. When I wrote this, my iPhone 7 with iOS 10.2 flatly refused to accept setting the date beyond 29 January 2038. Any attempt to do that just ended up with the device going back to 1 January that year. Officially, iOS 10 is 64 bit, and the device definitely supports long timestamps, but it looks like someone decided to disable going over the event horizon to prevent third-party software from blowing up.

Unfortunately, with the pace of technology these days, longevity is very low on the list of priorities for software design. But when specialist computers need higher precision than seconds, the digital apocalypse can come in a matter of months, as the next story shows.

HAVE YOU TURNED YOUR DREAMLINER OFF AND ON AGAIN?

In September 2004, Hamid Ghaffari was watching dots move around a computer screen. Working for the Los Angeles Air Route Traffic Control Center in Palmdale, California, USA, he was one of a handful of people responsible for getting everyone inside those dots on the ground safely. Around 5pm local time on Tuesday the 14th, two dots started coming dangerously close. Ghaffari tapped the touch screen of the Voice Switching and Control System (VSCS) to alert the pilots, but the system did not respond. 'You could see airplanes getting awfully close but you're powerless', Ghaffari later recounted in an interview for IEEE Spectrum.

The VSCS system usually allows traffic controllers to talk to airplane crews, but that Tuesday had decided to take a coffee break. The backup system had decided to join in as well. The Palmdale centre lost all contact with 400 airplanes flying across 460,000 square kilometres of air space over four US states. Soon, four other pairs of dots started coming closer than they should. Controllers scrambled to find alternative ways to talk to pilots. They used personal mobile phones to reach out to friends and colleagues working in other control centres. Some called the airlines directly, asking them to alert the crews. Luckily, the day ended without collisions.

The Federal Aviation Administration (FAA) review, published the next day, sounded like something out of The IT Crowd comedy show. It was all a human error, and someone had just forgotten to turn the system off and turn it on again.

Sure, anyone who has ever owned a PC knows that rebooting is the universal way to get rid of uninvited gremlins, but you'd expect that safety-critical systems have better control in place. And, in fact, the VSCS did have something designed to control it. A year before the incident, the Palmdale centre installed the VSCS Control Subsystem Upgrade or, with a recursive acronym, VCSU. The VCSU continually ran tests on the VSCS to ensure that the backup system took over if the primary system got stuck. But people at Harris Corporation, which designed the VSCS and VSCU, failed to consider the famous question asked by the Roman poet Juvenal: who watches the watchmen?

The VSCU used a 32-bit timer, counting down in milliseconds from the largest available value. In effect, this meant that the counter only worked for about 50 days. The timer was supposed to automatically reset itself when it reached zero, but nobody bothered to check that it did. And so, upon counting down to zero on 14 September, the VCSU went into a spasm. False results are worse than a total breakdown in safety-critical systems, so when the VCSU could no longer run tests on the VSCS, it just shut the VSCS down. When the backup system came online, the VCSU shut that one down for good measure as well.

The FAA did run a long test in the field and realised that the system crashed every 50 days, but didn't know why. Therefore they recommended that all centres restart their control units once a month. In fateful September 2014, someone just forgot to press Ctrl-Alt-Delete.

An unexpected zero easily makes computers go crazy. Zero is not valid for some numerical operations, such as division, but happens infrequently enough so people forget to test for it. The USS navy cruiser Yorktown famously froze when a technician entered a zero by mistake into one of the control parameters in 1997. The ship's computer network crashed and the crew lost control of the propulsion system for two and a half hours.

Another reason why zero might cause problems is that one system might use it to signal missing information, and another might consume it as the actual value. Nigel and Linda Brotherton from Roughlee in the UK got a shocking surprise from their electricity provider nPower in 2014, when their bill increased from £87 to £500 million. To make things easier for the elderly couple, nPower proposed taking £53,480,062.00 a month from their bank account. It turned out that the electricity meter was wired incorrectly, and always showed zero. When the meter reader entered zero into the system, the computers assumed that the meter display cycled over the available digits, and calculated a bill for the full capacity of the measuring equipment.

Getting to zero is often a consequence of resource depletion, something that plagues computers designed for long autonomous operations, such as the VCSU control system. This is because resource issues aren't noticeable over a short period of time, but they build up through extended usage. Most software testing needs to happen in a limited time span, much shorter than the normal operating cycle of such systems, so temporal problems tend to go unnoticed until it's too late.

Luckily, the civil aviation authorities take safety more seriously than software manufacturers do, so they actually run tests over an extended period. In 2015, for example, the US FAA issued a warning about the Boeing flagship, the 787 Dreamliner. Due to a software bug, the power generators would shut down after 248 days of continuous work. The cause was a timer in the generator control units, that would run out of available numbers, quite similar to the VCSU. The Dreamliner has four generators, and if they were all powered on at the same time, the airplane would lose electricity completely after 248 days of work, leading to a total loss of control. Thanks to the diligence of the FAA, this problem was caught in a laboratory condition, not mid-air. While Boeing worked on a software patch, the recommendation to all airlines operating the Dreamliners was to turn the generators off and turn them on again every six months.

Resource depletion problems can be especially vicious when a computer system enters an unusually long usage period for the first time.

For example, during Operation Desert Storm, the US military deployed Patriot missile defence systems to protect personnel in Saudi Arabia. The army had never used those systems in the field for extended periods before the war in Iraq. On 25 February 1991, the Patriot system operating at Dhahran, Saudi Arabia, launched a missile to intercept an incoming Scud and missed. This Iraqi Scud hit the army barracks, killing 28 soldiers. The US General Accounting Office report explained that the error was caused by loss of precision that built up over time.

The Patriot weapons-tracking systems used 24 bits of data to predict where to look for enemy missiles, and relied on the velocity of the tracked object and the timestamps from the radars. The longer the system kept running, the larger the timestamps and the less precision 24 bits of data offered. Combined with the fact that the Scuds were tactical ballistic missiles moving at Mach 5 (3750 mph), this meant that the system could only effectively defend against Scuds for the first eight hours of work. By the time the incident occurred, the weapons-control system had been running for more than 100 hours. Ironically, several weeks before that, the Israeli army warned its US counterparts that Patriots have to be rebooted frequently.

When the Palmdale centre system went berserk, at least it had the decency to commit suicide instead of giving out false data, so people had to start panicking and find alternative solutions. Had the Patriot system in Dhahran shut down completely, someone would have noticed the problem on time.

With modern computers, the danger of the entire system going down is generally well understood, and most critical applications have redundancies in place to deal with that. A part of the system going crazy, however, is a completely different story.

FREE MONEY SATURDAY

Wauwatosa is a quiet town on the western edge of Milwaukee. Named after the Potawatomi word for firefly, the town is rarely in the news. The 50,000 residents of Wauwatosa are predominantly middle class, and the town is home to several colleges and universities. The most notable event is usually when the local college wrestling team wins the Wisconsin title, which it's done for seven years in a row.

Wrestling in Wauwatosa took on a completely new scale on 24 November 2007, dubbed 'free money Saturday'. Police were called to the local Kmart store at around 11 am to stop a large fight that stretched from the parking lot all the way to the counters inside the store. And it was all caused by a computer glitch...

In the mid-2000s, large retailers around the world were discovering the benefits of big data. Store cards offer a quick and easy way to track customer purchases and collect data for statisticians to explore. Kmart ran a promotion offering $10 instant credit to anyone who successfully applied for a store card. For most Kmarts it was business as usual, but the Wauwatosa store for some reason instantly approved all applications. Not just that, but instead of the promised $10, people got up to $4,000 credit which they could spend immediately.

Word spread so quickly that the Wauwatosa Kmart store ran out of application forms. One enterprising Wisconsinite drove to a neighbouring Kmart, picked up a bunch of credit forms, and sold them in front of the Wauwatosa store for $20 each. Employees were ill-equipped to deal with such a gold rush, so a huge crowd quickly built up in the store. Two women started to fight, several men joined in, and the venue quickly became the scene of the biggest wrestling match in recent history. A Kmart employee was pushed through a glass display case, prompting other employees to call in the cavalry. When the police finally responded, it took a dozen patrol cars to calm things down.

The 'free money Saturday' incident nicely illustrates what happens when one system in a large chain decides to go rogue. Had all Kmart stores been affected, the problem would probably have been spotted sooner and the Wauwatosa shop wouldn't have been so overrun by enthusiastic customers. It's likely that nobody would have had their nose broken or earrings pulled or been pushed through glass. Still, because the crowd started filling up the store, very few actually got to use all that free credit, so the financial damage from the incident was relatively low.

Kmart was somewhat lucky that it was humans who responded to its enticing offer. The real mess happens when computers join in the gold rush. Knight Capital discovered that on 1 August 2012, in an incident that many financial analysts labelled a meltdown. Knight Capital was one of the key brokers on the New York Stock Exchange and wanted to play a big role in the newly introduced Retail Liquidity Program (RLP). The RLP enabled brokers to offer their retail clients prices that were fractions of cents better than the ones on the exchange. With miniscule gains on each trade, efficient execution is key to actually making money. Knight built a custom software system called SMARS to automate the trading. SMARS broke down retail orders into small chunks and predicted when it was best to send individual parts to the exchange to make the most money. Unfortunately, during a software update, someone forgot to install the new version on one of the eight computers used by SMARS. While processing 212 small retail orders, the eighth system didn't know when to stop, and kept enthusiastically approving trades long after a whole order was complete.

Similar to the Wauwatosa Kmart, the rogue system drew a big crowd. The error was spotted in less than an hour, but this time the algorithms were on the other side. Knight lost fractions of cents on each trade, but after buying and selling more than $6 billion of shares in 45 minutes, the costs added up to over $460 million. The blunder led to major price changes for shares in over 100 companies, a further punishment of $12 million by the Securities and Exchange Commission (SEC), the collapse of the Knight Capital stock price, and ultimately the departure of Knight's CEO. An emergency rescue investment saved Knight, but shareholders at the time lost 73% of the company.

Knight's primary risk-monitoring tool relied entirely on human interaction. Swamped with such a high volume of incoming trades, the monitoring system displayed delayed results, which is why it took so long for someone to raise an alarm. Given that one of the eight systems was the cause of the issue, and that it wasn't even running the correct version of the software, it's likely that Knight's engineers wasted time by investigating and shutting down systems that were actually working correctly.

Both Knight Capital and Kmart blindly trusted all their systems to work the same, and a single malfunctioning system caused a lot of damage. These stories illustrate how critical it is to monitor not just the effects of the whole automated process, but also the individual collaborators in the pipeline.

The SEC investigation blamed Knight Capital for not having automated risk controls, coming to the same conclusion as many other stories in this book. Automated decision making needs independent, automated oversight, otherwise it can run in a wrong direction incredibly quickly.

MR TEST

An ominous preview of Knight Capital's meltdown happened a whole year earlier, illustrating another key risk for automated decision systems. One of Knight's primary sources of revenue was market making for many smaller electronically traded funds. Market makers play a crucial role in financial exchanges by guaranteeing to buy or sell at a certain price, effectively ensuring that someone is always interested in matching an offer for less popular financial instruments. Knight Capital was a key player in one of the biggest stock exchanges in the world, so it had to ensure that its systems could continue working even in the event of data centre problems. In October 2011, Knight decided to test its disaster recovery plans. The test happened over a weekend, outside normal working hours, and was a success.

Market making is a high-volume business, mostly automated, so the engineers used a large set of test data to simulate a relevant flow of trading requests. Everything worked well, and people went home knowing that their recovery procedures could survive even a small disaster. Inadvertently, however, a disaster had been triggered for the next day. Someone had forgotten to remove the test data after the experiment. When trading resumed on Monday morning, Knight's computers continued to use the test data to match offers from the exchange. As a result, Knight lost more than US$7 million before someone spotted what was going on.

Although leaving test data in the real system for Knight was a mistake, software is often built to support running tests alongside real work. The more complex a system, the more likely it is to break at the seams. Having some way to place a test order is a cheap and effective way to check that everything is working, effectively putting some much needed automated oversight around algorithmic decision making. To make that idea work, however, it's critical to actually recognise the test cases.

Computers at Hartsfield–Jackson International Airport in Atlanta failed to spot the test on 19 April 2006, causing travel chaos around the world. In order to prove that the security systems and staff are not asleep, the luggage X-ray machine at the airport occasionally shows images of suspicious devices. Normally, the computer identifies the suspect device and, a few moments later, warns that the alarm is part of a test. However, that Wednesday, a computer failed to identify a test case. The Transportation Security Administration agent screening luggage noticed something that looked like a bomb, but couldn't find a bag that matched the image. He alerted a supervisor, and the two of them went through all the luggage on the conveyor belt again. The test bag invented by a computer wasn't there, of course. This was too strange to ignore, so the two of them escalated the problem to the security director, who decided to call the Atlanta police bomb squad. Passengers had to evacuate the terminal, and all flights were grounded for two hours. Hartsfield–Jackson International is the busiest airport in the world, so the delayed flights caused a knock-on effect and disrupted travel around the world.

Test data problems can stay under the radar for a long time. The US Securities and Exchange Commission fined Citigroup more than $7 million in 2016 because of a software glitch that caused the Global Markets division of the bank to incorrectly report regulatory data for 15 years. Citigroup Global Markets assigned test trades to special bank branch codes, ranging from 089 to 100. In 1999, the bank changed from purely numeric to alphanumeric branch codes. Some real branches had codes starting with the number 10 and followed by a letter, but the regulatory reporting software incorrectly assumed they were just tests and decided not to include any related trades in the reports.

People sometimes make up special cases for testing that couldn't possibly happen in real life, but make wrong assumptions about the world. James Bach got a parking ticket from the city of Everett on 16 December 2010, although he'd never parked in Everett. A county clerk confirmed that the ticket was in the system, but was confused by the case number. All tickets in Everett start with the number 10, but this one was 111111111. It turned out that the city of Everett had started using a new automated ticketing system just a few days before the alleged violation. Someone had obviously tried it out by issuing a made-up ticket that was easy to type in. That's why the case number was all 1s. To ensure the ticket was clearly flagged as a test case, the tester issued it for the licence plate TESTER. Bach, a well-known software testing consultant and author, actually has a custom licence plate matching exactly that name. Luckily the clerk quickly recognised the error, and a judge dismissed the case.

The way to avoid such tunnel vision caused by idealistic data is to test software upgrades using real-world examples. However, this approach can also create huge problems if test cases are not clearly identified.

On 16 March 2010, New York police raided a house in Marine Park in Brooklyn. The house had been raided more than 50 times in the previous eight years, so New York Police Department officers were prepared for heavy resistance. Instead, they found only Rose and Walter Martin, both over 80 years old.

The Martins had got used to the police banging on their doors, sometimes up to three times a week. On paper, the address looked like a hotbed of crime, but in fact this was all caused by a software test gone wild. In 2002, the police had used the Martins' address as part of a random data sample to test a new software system, but forgot to remove the test records afterwards. As a result, officers from all over New York started showing up in Marine Park looking for suspects.

In 2007, Rose wrote about the harassment to the Police Commissioner, Ray Kelly, warning that her husband's blood pressure problems could lead to a heart attack if the house was raided again. Commissioner Kelly ordered investigators to remove the Martins' address from their systems, but this turned out to be more difficult than expected. By that time, records had already been exchanged with many other police systems and copied into lots of different places. After the raid in 2010, Commissioner Kelly visited the Martins personally to apologise. Instead of trying to clean up test data further, police officials flagged the address with an alert, so that officers have to double-check any future visit with their superiors. It was easier to change the police process than to fix a software test data problem.

The problem with test cases co-existing with real data gets even weirder when several systems need to talk to each other, because tests in one system are not recognised in another. This was the case of James Test, whose flight booking with American Airlines kept disappearing into a void. 'The booking would last only long enough to process my credit card, then fade to just a test', complained Mr Test to The Wall Street Journal. Jeff Sample ran into a similar problem caused by disagreements between the computer systems of his travel agent, an airline in Argentina, and a bank. The airline processed his flight booking from Buenos Aires to Patagonia, and took the payment from his credit card, but another system then falsely flagged it as a test case and deleted the ticket. Even worse, the flight booking system no longer recognised the card charge, so Sample had problems getting a refund.

Sometimes, the only way to inspect a complex computer system is to allow special test cases to exist alongside real data. But this approach can backfire badly if the tests end up matching any real-world usage. This problem is particularly problematic if test data can also be used for authentication, as the next story shows.

FIVE BLANKS HIT THE TARGET

The city of Great Falls in Montana, USA, lies between the Great Plains and Rocky Mountains, close to some stunning scenery. There are five nearby waterfalls on the Missouri River, each powering a hydroelectric dam, earning Great Falls the nickname Electric City. The largest buffalo jump cliff in the world, in the First Peoples Buffalo Jump State Park, lies nearby. Native populations used the jump for thousands of years to hunt wild cattle from the plains, by making them stampede over the cliff. The Blackfoot Indians called the place Pishkun, meaning 'deep kettle of blood'. The area was part of the unincorporated frontier until 1854, because the nearby waterfalls marked the end of the navigable section of the Missouri River. Frequent clashes between explorers and native residents were only partially resolved by the notorious Treaty of Hellgate, plagued by cross-cultural miscommunication and mistranslations. With such a combination of violent history and high-voltage electricity, it's no wonder the city was chosen to be ground zero of the first recorded zombie apocalypse.

On 11 February 2013, the 50,000 residents of Great Falls were warned by the local TV station KRTV that 'dead bodies are rising from the grave and attacking the living'. The warning was distributed as a scrolling alert on TV screens through the Emergency Alert System, designed to allow the president of the

USA to break into TV broadcasts and announce a national crisis. Warning the public that the zombies were extremely dangerous and should not be approached or apprehended, the message also reached other TV stations in Montana and in states including Michigan, Utah and New Mexico, even as far as California. Luckily, at least according to the National Post, the damage was limited to just a few phone calls to the police asking whether guns are adequate protection against the undead.

The Montana zombie apocalypse spoof had quite wide reach, however. Cindy Paavola, from for the University of Northern Michigan, whose college TV station also carried the zombie warning, said the source was outside the USA. Given the importance of the Emergency Alert System, it was supposed to be resilient against amateur spoofing attacks. After an investigation, it turned out that Monroe Electronics' One-Net E189 Emergency Alert System devices included a 'shared private root SSH key in publicly available firmware images'. In plain English, that's a universal back-door key.

Although this fake alert is probably one of the most amusing examples of abusing default manufacturer keys, it's hardly the only case. Shortly after Donald Trump's inauguration, dozens of short-range radio stations throughout the USA started playing an anti-Trump song, the name of which is too offensive to print in a nice book such as this. The cause wasn't a sudden coordinated rebellion by small TV station owners, but a default password in Barix Exstreamer radio broadcasting devices.

The infamous Mirai botnet attack on 21 October 2016 was the largest recorded denial-of-service strike in history, at least at the time when I wrote this book. Roughly 100,000 devices generated 1.2Tbps of traffic, making Netflix, Twitter, Spotify, CNN, PayPal and many other high profile websites inaccessible. According to the security researcher Graham Cluley, the root cause was about 60 default passwords in poorly protected Internet digital video recorders and cameras.

A simple administrative account is often necessary for testing, but leaving it in software intended for consumers is just asking for trouble. In February 2016, IDG reported how a research group had discovered 46,000 Internet-connected cameras and digital recorders that could be accessed using a single password, 519070. The problematic password couldn't even be changed by the owners of the devices. And, in January 2016, Lenovo was forced to issue emergency security fixes for its file-sharing application after it emerged that the software came with the universal password 12345678.

The software development blunders described in this book often ended up causing harm to people and costing a lot of money. To end on a more positive note, consider this example of hard-coded administrative password that brought someone joy. Similar to many other children, Kristoffer von Hassel got hooked on video games. With ubiquitous gaming channels on YouTube, children today learn about new games quickly, even those that aren't really suitable for young players. Kristoffer's father caught him one day in 2014 playing games restricted to children far above his age, and forced him to reveal how that was possible. After a bit of interrogation, Kristoffer caved in.

Kristoffer noticed that his father could play restricted games, so when his parents were out, he tried to log in to his father's Xbox Live account. After several wrong password guesses, the games console showed the verification screen, where Kristoffer was supposed to enter a special code. Trying to go back, Kristoffer pressed in the space key five times and, to his amazement, gained access. 'I was like ... yeah!', said Kristoffer about his eureka moment to a CNN journalist. The father, of course, reported the problem to Microsoft. It turned out that five blanks was a leftover test password that anyone could use to sign in to any account. Microsoft awarded Kristoffer free games, and included him in the list of March 2014 security researchers who'd contributed to its products. At the time, Kristoffer was just five years old, which makes him the youngest successful hacker in history.

THE INVERSE MONKEY RULE

Émile Borel proposed the famous infinite monkeys theorem in 1913, suggesting that given infinite time and attempts, monkeys would come up with the works of Shakespeare. Borel's theorem is a nice illustration of statistics and calculus, but in practice the probability is infinitely small. On the other hand, inverting the subjects and the outcome gives us something a lot more practical, in much less time: the Inverse Monkey Rule.

Smart people, hitting keys intentionally on a computer keyboard, given just a few months, will almost surely produce some kind of monkey crap.

Perfect software is impossible. Without an infinite amount of time and infinite knowledge, people will always make mistakes. But we don't have to repeat predictable errors.

This part will help you avoid the mistakes that other people made to deserve a mention in this book. It contains a set of ideas on how to avoid similar problems. Please note that this isn't a comprehensive list of test cases or a full testing strategy, just a quick digest of the stories in this book. Use it as a check-list along with your other tools, and as an inspiration when looking for more ideas.

PERSONAL NAMES

Personal identifiers such as names are a crucial piece of our identities. Many software problems result from a fundamental conflict between the two key aspects of names. On one hand, names are personal, so they carry a lot of cultural and family heritage, tracing back to a time long before computers. Specific spellings, accents and parts of names have meaning and can't just be simplified or changed to make processing easier. On the other hand, useful computer identifiers need to be standardised and easy to store and process. In many cases, various software systems need to agree on someone's identity. All those systems were designed by different people, working under specific constraints, making their own assumptions. That's why small inconsistencies and bugs in handling names in one component can easily create a mess in collaborating systems.

Here are some often-overlooked oddities of personal names, which you should remember when designing software:

Single-letter names aren't always initials, so it's bad practice to use length checks to prevent people from entering initials (*Stephen O, A Martinez, O Rissei*).

There's no universally acceptable standard for maximum name length. The International Civil Aviation Organization (ICAO) allows up to 64 characters per name. Many governments today limit registered baby names to those that fit on a passport, which may be up to 40 letters. Of course, different governments have different standards. Also, people born before machine readable passports weren't subject to that restriction. Some names can get very long (e.g. *Christodoulopoulos, Srinivasaraghavan, StopFortnumAndMasonFoieGras, Wolfeschlegelsteinhausenbergerdorff, Rhoshandiatellyneshiaunneveshenk,*

Keihanaikukauakahihulihe'ekahaunaele). Double-barrelled surnames can also get quite long (e.g. *Plunkett-Ernle-Erle-Drax*).

Names aren't permanent, and in most countries people can easily change their names as many times as they want.

Names don't just consist of letters. They can contain accents and apostrophes (*O'Stephen*, *Keihanaikukauakahihulihe'ekahaunaele*), dots (*GoVeg.com*), dashes (*Thurman-Busson*), numbers (*Number 16 Bus Shelter, Jon Blake Cusack 2.0*) and probably some other classes of symbols. It's best not to assume any specific character set for validity checks.

People don't always have a given name and a surname. Some people are mononymic – they have only a single name (e.g. *They, Teller, Naqibullah*). It's best not to ask for first and last name separately. When communicating with external systems, make sure you can handle cases in which one of those two fields is missing.

There's no universally accepted standard for working with mononymic names. Many government systems require first and last names to be recorded separately, and some will set mononymic names as the given name, some as the surname. Some use the mononymic name for both fields (*Neli Neli*). When matching names against external sources, consider that the sources might be using different schemes for single names. Some countries use markers such as FNU, LNU or XXX for the other name when recording mononymic people. Detect those markers and consider them when matching or validating external records, so you don't end up interpreting them as given names (*No Name Given Sandhya*). But don't assume these are always markers (someone can theoretically change their name to *XXX*).

People don't always have just one or two given names and surnames. *Tracy Nelson* has 138 middle names. A nice example is *Rosalind Arusha Arkadina Altalune Florence Thurman-Busson*. For a good edge case, remember *James Dr No From Russia with Love*

Goldfinger Thunderball You Only Live Twice On Her Majesty's Secret Service Diamonds Are Forever Live and Let Die The Man with the Golden Gun The Spy Who Loved Me Moonraker For Your Eyes Only Octopussy A View to a Kill The Living Daylights Licence to Kill Golden Eye Tomorrow Never Dies The World Is Not Enough Die Another Day Casino Royale Bond.

Test, Sample and many other common words are also valid names. Just because a user's surname is Test doesn't mean that it's actually a test account. When testing, avoid using specific names to mark example data, because real users might get caught by this as well.

Fictional character names aren't necessarily always fake (Superman Wheaton, Buzz Lightyear, Darth Vader). Names that are also those of popular brands aren't always fake either (*Facebook Jamal Ibrahim, Google Kai*). Common English (or any other language) words or phrases in a name don't necessarily make it fake (*Elaine Yellow Horse, Above Znoneofthe*).

TIME

Time is a quite a tricky subject for software. Most people have an established intuitive perception about time, so it's easy to oversimplify and overlook edge cases. In addition, although the concept of time is simple, there are at least three distinct versions of it, and they aren't always synchronised.

Cosmic time is passing in the real world without any care for humans. It's governed by the laws of physics. Although Einstein famously declared it to be relative, for most purposes it's the same everywhere on planet Earth. It's also continuous and, except in bad science fiction, always moves in a single direction.

Elapsed time deals with periods between two reference points in cosmic time. This is the time we can measure, and deals with periods such as seconds. Elapsed time doesn't have any notion of midnight, summer or Tuesday next week. This type of time is a human invention, but apart from someone choosing the two reference points for measurement, it doesn't depend on humans. Instead, it depends on the recording machinery. For computers today, this mostly means that elapsed time isn't continuous, but discrete, in increments of milliseconds. Theoretically, it should be the same everywhere on Earth, but practically it's not. Measuring devices use different precision and accuracy. Your computer and your mobile phone may measure the same period differently, and they both diverge slightly from NIST-F1, the atomic clock that controls the official time in the USA. Lastly, elapsed time isn't infinite. It's subject to the capacity of measurement equipment, which is why many older computers can't see beyond 2038.

Clock time is the one used for calendars, to guide our daily lives, schedule meetings and keep society synchronised. Clock time deals with concepts such as 14:45pm, wake-up alarms, and beer o'clock. It's different in different places of the world, driven by solar cycles, the Earth's rotation, and the needs of the communities living in a particular area. It's a uniquely human thing, subject to politics, government conventions and manipulation. It can jump ahead, move backwards, stall or stretch.

Most of the time, excuse the pun, the three types are the same for all practical purposes. But the problems start when they suddenly diverge, even if only for a moment.

Here are some commonly overlooked quirks of time that cause problems:

Days aren't always exactly 86,400 seconds long. Leap seconds can make a day one second longer. (*31 December 2016* had a leap second.)

Scheduling future events by using elapsed time is dangerous. For example, 'same time tomorrow' isn't always 24 hours away. Daylight saving can shift the clock. People might travel into a different time zone. The longer the period until the scheduled time, the more chance of a mess.

Coordinated Universal Time (UTC) and Greenwich Mean Time (GMT) time zones aren't always the same. They can drift by up to 0.9 seconds. That's why leap seconds exist.

Leap seconds don't necessarily have to be positive. If the Earth's rotation required it, it would theoretically be possible to introduce a negative leap second. This has never happened so far – but once it does, better stay home that day.

Years aren't always 365 days long. Remember the occasional 29 February.

Leap years don't happen every four years. Three out of four end-of-century years don't have a leap day.

Clock time doesn't always go forwards. Daylight saving can make it jump backwards. Remeber *Samuel Peterson* who was born both 30 minutes before and after his twin brother *Ronan*.

Computers couldn't care less about clock time, they only deal with elapsed time. Applying clock time arithmetic to elapsed time often leads to problems. For example, adding one month to the current time doesn't produce a period of exactly one month in clock time. Time zones, different numbers of days in a month and other exceptions can cause wrong calculations.

Clock time and elapsed time don't always move by the same amount. Daylight saving can create big gaps.

Daylight saving time isn't applied consistently across all countries, or even within a single country. For example, most of the USA observes daylight saving time, but Hawaii does not. In Australia, New South Wales observes daylight saving time, but Queensland does not.

The daylight saving time schedule isn't fixed. It's a political agreement, subject to change. For example, Israel synchronised time zone changes with the east of Europe in 2013, moving the end of summer time from early September to late October.

Elapsed time isn't always positive. Most computers represent dates before 1970 as negative numbers. More importantly, midnight UK time on *1 January 1970* gets recorded as 0.

Unlike cosmic and clock time, elapsed time isn't infinite. Check the numeric limits of your date records, and test around those. For example, for typical 32-bit dates, test for dates before 1970 and after February 2038.

Missing or invalid time might mask itself as 1 January 1970 or 31 December 1969, especially if you're using third-party components outside your control.

NUMBERS

Although modern software applications can appear to be processing text or displaying dates or emojis, in fact computers only deal with numbers. Bad assumptions about the mapping between numbers and contextual information such as shopping cart quantities often lead to trouble. Some values, such as a pack of cigarettes costing $23,148,855,308,184,500, are obviously wrong to humans, but to a computer that's just a number like any other. Some perfectly valid numerical values, such as 0, might make no sense when used as contextual information, such as characters on screen. Some contextual information requires a particular sequence of numbers, such as Unicode combinations, but computers will happily store and transmit invalid numerical sequences.

Here are some ideas around amounts and quantities to remember when developing software:

Don't assume you can apply trivial mathematical rounding to fractional amounts. There are specific rounding and truncation rules for financial information, and they vary by country.

Not all currencies use two decimals. For example, *Japanese yen* don't use decimal fractions. *Kuwaiti dinar* have three decimals.

Try amounts with and without decimal places, and with varying number of decimals.

There's no universally agreed standard for writing currency amounts (or if there is, normal people don't obey it). Expect users to input currency amounts inconsistently. To a person, 5000, $5,000, $5 000 and $5,000.00 mean the same thing. If you want consistent information, make sure to check for a particular format.

People in different countries use different separators for thousands and decimals. The US number 1,234.56 would be 1 234,56 in France. Don't just remove all the commas before turning a string into a number.

Try negative values where they're not expected (*–1 books*).

Don't assume quantities always need to be positive. In some business domains, it's perfectly acceptable to have a negative quantity (for example, to mark items returned by customers).

Avoid using special values to mark missing information (such as *0* or *No Plates*), as this can be interpreted as the actual value by someone else.

Avoid marking test data with special values (such as having a surname *Test*), as this can easily create false positives. It's best to have specially identified accounts for testing, which you can later clean up.

Explore rounding strategies, especially with things that accumulate over time. Small rounding errors can create a big mess.

With Unicode, memory length and screen length aren't necessarily related. Some Unicode symbols are very long ((*0xFDFD*), some are invisible (*0x200B*), and some combine with previous characters (*0x0597*).

Check how the contextual data gets recorded and test around the corresponding numerical boundaries. For example, test what happens when the timer reaches the end of a 32-bit number range.

The number 0 is often interpreted as false information or missing data, or is just not expected in mapping to contextual values. Test what happens when your data maps to 0. Remember the 787 Dreamliner engines that would shut down when the control timer reached zero.

PROCESS AUTOMATION

Computers excel at doing things fast, but there's a general trend of trusting them too much to do their work well. Small errors can pass undetected for a long time, accumulate and build up a time-bomb. Perhaps even worse, pointing the computer in a wrong direction and letting it run off can cause small oversights to quickly escalate into a major blunder.

Lots of things can cause bad automation, even with the best intentions of people building the software. Third-party systems can send invalid, unexpected data. Migrating a legacy database may uncover lots of unforeseen edge cases. One part of the system can decide to go rogue and disrupt everything around it.

Apart from having a crystal ball that can see into the future, the best way to stop bad automation is to create an automated system of oversight. Build up monitoring and alerting mechanisms that can spot when something out of the ordinary is happening, and get people in to investigate before it's too late.

Here are some ideas on keeping automation in check:

Testing with small samples often doesn't uncover all the data-driven issues of large legacy databases. If you're converting a legacy database, run some basic characterisation statistics on the converted data and check with the domain experts whether things look all right. Remember the *Grand Rapids hospital* update that declared 5% of the population dead overnight.

If your system is automatically processing financial transactions, put monitors in place to check for trends. Good candidates are the expected volume of fraud or number of purchases per hour. If things fall too far outside the expected range, alert a person

– even if things look as if they're in your favour. Remember the *610,000 Japanese yen* fat-finger error and *MiDAS* fiasco.

If your system is automatically changing some data, such as prices, put monitors in place to check that automated changes are inside a valid range. For example, alert a person if the price goes too low or too high. This will help you avoid cases such as the *28,639.14 Uber ride,* or Repricer Express *selling everything at $0.01.*

Put monitors in place to check whether one of your systems is behaving significantly differently from the rest. For example, if a single trading processor is running 90% of the volume, get someone to investigate why before it's too late. Remember how one of eight *Knight Capital SMARS* systems ran a previous version of the software and it almost bankrupted the company.

Consider that speeding up a single part of a process might create problems downstream. For example, increasing the capacity to send out customer notifications can overload your call centre and create more problems than it solves, such as in the *Centrelink robo-debt fiasco.*

If you're generating random outcomes and they need to fall within some expected business rules, make sure to check those rules before you publish the results. Random things are just that – random – and, in some cases, might be surprising. It's potentially better to alert a person, or even to crash the system, than to directly use such unexpected values. Remember the *Pepsi 349 lottery.*

If you ever use sample data to validate or monitor your software, make sure that your tests are clearly identified, isolated and don't end up matching any real-world cases. Remember *Jeff Sample* and the *50 police raids on Walter Martin's house.*

Biometry isn't necessarily unique. Unrelated people do look alike. Twins can trick smart photo algorithms or leave a similar voice signature; remember the *Kennedy sisters.*

Monitor whether third-party systems are sending you strange data. For example, check whether some values appear a lot more frequently than the others. This will help to identify special markers for missing or invalid records, in particular where blank values aren't allowed (remember the *NO PLATE* parking tickets). Make sure to check third-party data for more than one entity where you expect only one (remember *concurrent criminal sentences*).

Check whether data coming from third-party systems is out of the usual range. For example, flag a *payment request for $23,148,855,308,184,500.*

If you're sending important messages through a third-party system, don't just trust that the notifications are dispatched. Build a mechanism requiring recipients to confirm that the messages have actually been delivered. Not everyone will confirm, of course, but you will at least be able to monitor trends and see if something unexpected happens, such as 50,000 people mistakenly dropping off the system. Remember the *Queensland OneSchool police e-mails*.

If you're working on a system that's supposed to work unattended and autonomously, leave it running for a long period of time and check whether gremlins appear. And do consider shutting the whole system down if it is mission critical and loses the ability to control itself.

Whenever you're using a slowly depleting but limited resource, make sure to build in monitoring, and send alerts when it starts getting dangerously low. For example, if you're using a count-down timer, notify someone to restart it before it gets to zero. Don't just rely on a published procedure for people to follow, because they might forget or have higher priorities at the time when things become critical.

If you're using any kind of hard-coded accounts for development and testing, make sure they don't somehow find their way into production software. Remember *five blanks granting Xbox access*.

ADDRESSES

Postal addresses are an important link between the virtual realm of the Internet and the physical world. Apart from the obvious role in shipping the stuff people buy online, knowing users' addresses is also critical for calculating delivery prices, correctly accounting for tax, and applying territory-specific limitations.

But postal addresses often play three more roles in software, which they were never intended for. With the lack of globally unique personal identifiers, addresses are also used to distinguish between two people with the same name, especially in countries that don't have mandatory ID cards, such as the UK. Addresses also often serve as an additional piece of personal identification to match records from different systems, for example when banks check credit ratings. And parts of addresses, such as zip or post codes, are increasingly used as semi-secret information to prevent fraud, for example when verifying online credit card transactions.

For hundreds of years, postal delivery processes evolved to deal with inconsistent and incomplete addresses, but the new digital roles for address information require exact, precise and uniform data. Similar to names, the different conflicting roles of addresses create plenty of opportunities for software bugs.

Here are some often-overlooked facts that cause problems when handling addresses in software:

ZIP codes or post codes aren't mandatory. Some countries don't use post codes (*Fiji, UAE*).

Post code formats aren't permanent, they change over time. For example, Singapore used two digits in the '60s, four digits in the

'80s, and now uses six digits. Older records with post codes might use different formats from the current ones.

Some countries started using post codes relatively recently. For example, post codes were introduced in Ireland in 2014. For such cases, even though current addresses might have post codes, slightly older address records might not have that information.

Post codes aren't always consistently used, even within a single country. For example, Jamaica doesn't use post codes (the country tried to, but the system was suspended in 2007), but there are two-digit area codes for the capital, Kingston. China uses post codes, but Hong Kong does not.

There's no universally agreed length for post codes. For example, Austria and Switzerland use four-digit codes. The Faroe Islands use three-digit codes. Iran uses up to ten.

Post codes aren't just numeric; many countries use alphanumeric post codes. For example, *EC11AA* is a valid UK post code.

Post codes can contain spaces. For example, *EC1 1AA* is a common way of writing a post code in the UK.

Having the same or similar post codes doesn't necessarily imply physical proximity. For example, rural codes in New Zealand can be far apart.

Post codes aren't always the same in a city or area. In the UK, post codes are allocated to estates, blocks, buildings or even individual houses.

There's no universally agreed minimum or maximum length for location names, including for street names or city names. For example, *Llanfairpwllgwyngyllgogerychwyrndrobwllllantysiliogogogoch* is a place in Wales, *Y* is a place in France. There are six villages called *Å* in Norway.

IP addresses aren't a reliable link to a physical location. Although many home broadband subscribers now effectively have an allocated IP address, there are too many exceptions and ways to spoof this information.

Out of all the categories of problems, real-world rules around addresses seem to change the most frequently at the moment. The examples and edge cases listed above were correct when I wrote this in 2017, but do check.

As Porky Pig would say, 'That's all folks.' I hope these examples tickled your imagination, and that they'll inspire you to improve how you design, test and build software systems. If you'd like to dive into any of the stories mentioned in the book further, check out the articles and references on in following appendix.

APPENDIX: REFERENCES AND BIBLIOGRAPHY

This appendix contains a list of all the reference material, news reports, articles and papers used in the research for this book. If you're reading this in an electronic version, just click the links to open online resources. If you're reading this on paper, go to humansvscomputers.com to find an online, clickable version of this appendix.

LICENCE TO VOID

- Why California Needs a Temporary License Plate Program, Metropolitan Transport Commission, 2014
- What Not to Do After Your Driver's License Is Suspended, by Steve Harvey, LA Times, 8 September 2004
- Man with "XXXXXXX" number plate receives parking fines for every unidentified car in city, by Matthew Moore, The Telegraph, 21 October 2009
- Licensed to Bill, by David Mikkelson, Snopes, 30 October 1999
- People and Events, by Steve Harvey, LA Times, 11 October 1988
- 'No' Doesn't Always Mean 'No' on a Personalized License Plate, by Steve Harvey, LA Times, 2 September 2004

GET OUT OF JAIL FREE

- Failed parole policy threatens lives, neighborhoods, by Katharine Russ, LAPD City Watch, 3 August 2010
- Parolees rounded up for more supervision, by Jeff McDonald, The San Diego Union Tribune, 2 May 2010

- Justices, 5-4, Tell California to Cut Prisoner Population, by Adam Liptak, The New York Times, 23 May 2011
- Computer errors allow violent California prisoners to be released unsupervised, by Jack Dolan, Los Angeles Times, 26 May 2011
- Second homicide tied to Washington inmates released by mistake, by Lewis Kamb and Joseph O'Sullivan, The Seattle Times, 31 December 2015
- Prison Official in Washington State Resigns Over Early-Release Error, by Ashley Southall, The New York Times, 6 February 2016
- US prisoners released early by software bug, BBC News, 23 December 2015
- Why it took the state nearly 4 years to address prison-release error, by Tom James, Crosscut, 16 January 2016
- Prisoner mistakenly released early charged with killing teen, CBS News/Associated Press, 31 December 2015
- 'Pink-Panther-Räuber' in der Schweiz gefasst, Burgenland-News, ORF, 10 December 2014
- Prison error releases robber too early, The Local/Austrian Press Agency, 6 October 2014
- Murder suspect mistakenly released from L.A. County jail is captured, by James Queally and Cindy Chang, The Los Angeles Times, 8 February 2016
- 'On-the-run' inmate in cell, The Sentinel, 18 August 2008
- The human errors letting prisoners walk free, by Rohan Smith, News.com.au, 10 February 2016

-1 BOOKS

- Jeffrey Bezos, Washington Post's next owner, aims for a new 'golden era' at the newspaper, By Paul Farhi, The Washington Post, 3 September 2013
- Online Experimentation at Microsoft, Tonny Kohavi, Thomas Crook and others, Microsoft ThinkWeek paper, 2009
- One Click by Richard L. Brandt, Portfolio, ISBN 9781591843757, 27 October 2011

- Birth of a Salesman, by Richard L. Brandt, The Wall Street Journal, 15 October 2011
- Amazon Hacks, by Paul Bausch, O'Reilly Media, ISBN 978-0596005429, 30 August 2003
- Entering negative value in "Add Subscriptions" changes value to all available subscriptions/entitlements, Red Hat Bugzilla – Bug 1372002, 31 August 2016
- Node reservation argument should not be negative or invalid value, Red Hat Bugzilla – Bug 1320433, 23 March 2016
- When a purchase order is created with a negative quantity..., IBM Support IZ59497, 27 August 2009
- Negative "On Order" Quantity, Intuit Accountants Community, 10 January 2008

PEPSI 349

- Updated Keno Statement, Vernon A. Kirk, Delaware Lottery, 5 February 2016
- Delaware lottery glitch leads to $2M lawsuit, by Jessica Masulli Reyes, The News Journal/USA Today, 28 November 2016
- B.C. Lotto website glitch leads to $1M in retroactive winnings, CBC News, 9 July 2015
- Va. Lottery Winners: Don't Spend That Money Yet, By Michael Birnbaum, Washington Post, 21 October 2008
- Virginia Lottery to award partial prizes for faulty game, The Lottery Post, 31 October 2008
- Lottery glitch makes it harder to pick a winner, by Matthew Walberg, Chicago Tribune, 5 May 2012
- Washington Lottery Computer Glitch Turns Winner Into Loser, by John McKay, News Talk 870 AM KFLD, 4 January 2013
- Washington Lottery's Veterans Raffle falls far short of its goal, by Jordan Schrader, The Seattle Times, 3 January 2013
- Oops, wrong numbers: Louisiana Lottery says TV show erred, Washington Times/Associated Press, 13 March 2017
- Computer glitch voids green card lottery results, CNN, 14 May 2011

- Green card lottery: US reviews 'diversity visa' glitch, **BBC News**, 6 June 2011
- Bottle Cap Flap Riles the Masses, by Bob Drogin, **Los Angeles Times**, 26 July 1993
- Holders of '349' Pepsi-Cola crowns lose bid in Supreme Court, by Joamar Canlas, **The Manila Times**, 25 August 2005
- G.R. No. 146007, decision of the Philippines Supreme Court, in the case of Pepsi Cola Company vs Jaime Lacanilao
- SC decides in finality on 'Pepsi 349' case, **The Freeman**, 26 June 2006

THE HAUNTED FARM IN THE MIDDLE OF AMERICA

- How an internet mapping glitch turned a random Kansas farm into a digital hell, by **Kashmir Hill, Fusion**, 10 April 2016
- Why lost phones are traced to Christina Lee and Michael Saba's Atlanta house, **The Sydney Morning Herald**, 8 February 2016
- Kansas family sues mapping company for years of 'digital hell', by Olivia Solon, **The Guardian** 9 August 2016
- Montgomery school bus driver arrested on child-porn charges, by Robert Samuels, **The Washington Post**, 25 March 2011
- US couple sues IP mapping firm over 'digital hell' by **Kevin Rawlinson, BBC News**, 11 August 2016
- Kansas couple sues IP mapping firm for turning their life into a "digital hell", **Cyrus Farivar, Ars Technica**, 10 August 2016

THE OLDER YOUNGER BROTHER

- Queensland Optus mobile phones change to daylight saving time, by **Natalie Bochenski, The Sydney Morning Herald**, 14 January 2015
- Mobile phone glitch: Daylight saving error wakes Queensland Optus and Virgin customers an hour early, by **Emilie Gramenz and Matt Eaton, ABC Radio Brisbane**, 14 January 2015
- Council chiefs left red-faced after TWO clocks are put forward instead of back by contractors, by Todd Fitzgerald, **Manchester**

Evening News, 30 October 2016

- Device exploded in bomber's face after he 'forgot about clocks changing', The Telegraph, 2 April 2014
- Meter fault gives free parking, by Chris Morris, Otago Daily Times, 1 May 2010
- Apology after some Dunedin parking meters not adjusted for daylight savings, by Hamish McNeilly, Stuff NZ, 26 September 2016
- Risks to the public in computers and related systems, by Peter G. Neurnann, ACM SIGSOFT Software Engineering Notes, vol. 17, No. 3, July 1992, ISSN:0163-5948
- Notices cancelled following glitch, New Zealand Police, 20 May 2015
- Apple iPhone 4 alarm clock bug makes scores late for work, by Claudine Beaumont, The Telegraph, 1 November 2010
- Israel does the time warp; daylight savings glitch wreaks havoc, by Niv Elis, Jerusalem Post, 8 September 2013
- Second Twin Born as Daylight Saving Time Ends Winds Up Older Than His Brother, by Caitlin Nolan, Inside Edition, 11 November 2016

HUBERT BLAINE WOLFE+585, SR

- A Third Survey of Domestic Electronic Digital Computing Systems: IBM 7070 Section., Ballistic Research Laboratories (BRL). Report No. 1961
- What's in a name, 666 Letters, plus 26 Given Names, by Norman Goldstein, The Free-Lance Star/ Associated Press, 25 June 1964
- Hawaiian woman with 36-character last name wins ID card battle, The Guardian, 31 December 2013
- Passenger and airport data interchange standards, version 13.1, ICAO, October 2013
- Machine Readable Travel Documents, ICAO, Seventh Edition, 2015
- Name acceptability guidelines by the Australian Department of Foreign Affairs and Trade

- Form I-94 Arrival/Departure Record reference copy, U.S. Customs and Border Protection, 24 April 2014
- Government Data Standards Catalogue Volume 2 – Data Types Standards, issue 0.5, UK Cabinet Office
- What's in a name? John and Margaret Nelson obviously feel..., United Press International, 23 January 1986
- Are there any restrictions on names and titles?, UK Deed Poll office
- The name's Bond ... times 21, The Scotscman, 17 November 2006
- Why, O Why, Doesn't That Name Compute?, New York Times, 28 August 1991
- Emma's 14 Bond names, The Sun, 28th October 2012.

GOVEG.COM

- What's in a name? Ask GoVeg.com, by Nara Schoenberg, Chicago Tribune, 18 July 2003
- Man changes his name to Tyrannosaurus Rex because it's 'cooler' than his own, by Richard Hartley-Parkinson, Mail Online, 9 May 2012
- Woman Gets New Name On eBay, by Tatiana Morales, CBS/Associated Press, 30 March 2005
- Baby named Metallica rocks Sweden, BBC News, 4 April 2007
- Couple tries to name child '@', CNN/Reuters, 16 August 2007
- Is it a bird? Is it a plane? No, it's a baby.., Reuters, 8 August 2013
- 'Number 16 Bus Shelter', 'Violence' among kids registered names, NZ Herald, 24 July 2008
- US father names son 'Version 2.0', BBC News, 2 February 2004

THEY

- Missouri man legally changes his name to 'They', USA Today/Associated Press, 23 September 2004
- In Search of Achmad Sukarno, by Steven Drakeley,

University of Western Sydney, Asia Reconstructed: Proceedings of the 16th Biennial Conference of the ASAA, 2006 (ISBN 9780958083737)

- U Thant, United Nations Secretary-General web site
- Flight Booking - Passenger has single name only in Passport, Trip Advisor, 2 May 2015
- How Do You Do, FNU? Some in U.S. Handle Just One Name, by Miriam Jordan, The Wall Street Journal, 21 March 2016

THE FOUR-LETTER N-WORD

- How to pass "Null" (a real surname!) to a SOAP web service in ActionScript 3?, Stack Overflow, 16 December 2010
- A few years ago I ordered a custom license plate 'NULL', Hacker News, 26 March 2016
- Null References: The Billion Dollar Mistake, by Tony Hoare, InfoQ, 25 August 2009
- Hello, I'm Mr. Null. My Name Makes Me Invisible to Computers, by Christopher Null, Wired Magazine, 5 November 2015
- These unlicky people have names that break computers, By Chris Baraniuk, BBC Future, 25 March 2016
- Cleverest con of all time? Man claims he gets free holidays and car rentals after changing his surname to 'Null', by Caroline McGuire, Daily Mail Online, 29 March 2016

FACEBOOK JAMAL IBRAHIM

- Australian with 'misleading' Facebook name thanks supporters, BBC News, 23 November 2015
- Vietnamese name man admits hoax in Facebook battle, BBC News, 25 November 2015
- A Gay Girl in Damascus becomes a heroine of the Syrian revolt, by Katherine Marsh, The Guardian, 6 May 2011
- Will gays be 'sacrificial lambs' in Arab Spring?, by Catriona Davies, CNN, 13 June 2011
- After Report of Disappearance, Questions About Syrian

American Blogger, by Robert Mackey and Liam Stack, The Lede/The New York Times, 7 June 2011

- 'Gay girl in Damascus' Syrian blogger allegedly kidnapped, by Elizabeth Flock, The Washington Post, 7 June 2011
- 'A Gay Girl in Damascus' comes clean, by Melissa Bell and Elizabeth Flock, The Washington Post, 12 June 2011
- Batman bin Suparman jailed in Singapore, BBC Trending, 12 November 2013
- 'Buzz Lightyear' fined £200 for speeding - in a CORSA, Sunday Express, 11 November 2016
- Baby named Metallica rocks Sweden, BBC News, 4 April 2007
- To Celebrate January 25 Revolution, Egyptian Man Names Daughter 'Facebook', by William Lee Adams, Time magazine, 21 February 2011
- The name's 7, iPhone 7: Ukrainian man changes name to win gadget, RT/Associated Press, 29 October 2016
- NY man legally changes name to 'Star Wars' villain, Associated Press, 21 December 2015
- Hello Mr Cheeseburger: name-changing hits record high, by Zachary Spiro, The Times, February 22 2016
- Meet the people who've given themselves crazy names by deed poll, by Julie McCaffrey, Mirror 1 November 2011
- Man Legally Changes Name to 'Above Znoneofthe' to Appear Last on Ballot, Katie Reilly, Time Magazine, 30 January 2016
- Teenager changes name to Captain Fantastic, by Chris Irvine, The Telegraph, 3 November 2008

TDCU 1ZZ

- Bill paves way for introduction of new 'Eircode' postcodes by Michael O'Regan, The Irish Times, 11 June 2015
- Your man with glasses letter reaches Buncrana man Barry Henderson, BBC News, 18 July 2015
- Beverly Hillsin postinumero 90 210 katoaa Oulusta, by Kari Sankala, Kaleva, 7 October 2009
- First postcode for remote UK isle, BBC News, 7 August 2005

LEAP YEAR HICAPS

- Excel incorrectly assumes that the year 1900 is a leap year, Microsoft Support Article ID 214326, 17 Dec 17, 2015
- Exchange Server 2007 and leap year day Feb 29 2008..., Microsoft Exchange Team Blog, 29 February 2008
- Yes, Microsoft Azure Was Downed By Leap-Year Bug, By Dan Goodin, Ars Technica/Wired, 1 March 2012
- Summary of Windows Azure Service Disruption on Feb 29th, 2012, Bill Laing, Microsoft Azure Blog, 9 March 2012
- Airport hiccup leaves 100s of passengers pantless, The Local, 1 March 2016
- Leap year glitch fixed on Sony Playstation 3, by Kristin Kalning, NBC News, 2 March 2010
- Microsoft Says Zune players working again, NBC News, 2 January 2009
- Schalttag-Problem legt Koffersoftware lahm, Der Spiegel, 29 February 2016
- Hundreds of passengers arrive at their destinations without their luggage after airport sorting device REFUSES to work because it didn't recognise the leap year, by Georgia Diebelius, Daily Mail, 2 March 2016
- Leap year blamed for HICAPS stumble by Chris Zappone, The Sydney Morning Herald, 29 February 2012
- TomTom sat-nav devices hit by GPS 'leap year bug', BBC News, 3 April 2012
- Montreal radio system also stymied by 'leap second' glitch that hit Ottawa, by Jon Willing, Ottawa Sun, 5 January 2017
- 'Leap Second' Bug Wreaks Havoc Across Web, by Cade Metz, Wired, 7 January 2012
- No, the Linux leap second bug WON'T crash the web, by Gavin Clarke, The Register, 9 January 2015
- Leap second hits Qantas air bookings, while Reddit and Mozilla stutter, by Charles Arthur, 2 July 2012
- Excel incorrectly assumes that the year 1900 is a leap year, Microsoft Knowledge Base article 214326, 17 December 2015

610,000 JPY

- UBS Warburg Stands to Lose Reputation Along With Millions After Dentsu Fiasco, by Jason Singer and Yumiko Ono, The Wall Street Journal, 3 December 2001
- Tokyo market chief quits over 'fat finger' trade, by Mariko Sanchanta, Financial Times, 20 December 2005
- 'Fat finger' trade costs Tokyo shares boss his job, by David McNeill, The Independent, 2 April 2009
- UBS Japan mistakenly places $31 bln bond trade, by Mariko Katsumura, Reuters, 25 February 2009
- $617 Billion in Japan Stock Orders Scrapped After Error, by Anna Kitanaka, Bloomberg, 1 October 2014

THE KENNEDY SISTERS FRAUD

- Local Twins Denied a Learner's Permit Because The DMV Can't Tell Them Apart, by Margaret-Ann Carter, WJBF-TV News Channel 6, 22 October 2015
- BBC fools HSBC voice recognition security system, by Dan Simmons, BBC News, 19 May 2017
- Caught in a dragnet, by Meghan E. Irons, The Boston Globe, 17 July 2011
- State scans Mass. license photos to find matches with suspects, By Matt Rocheleau, The Boston Globe, 20 December 2016
- Assisting Pathologists in Detecting Cancer with Deep Learning, by Martin Stumpe and Lily Peng, Google Research Blog, 3 March 2017
- Are Face-Detection Cameras Racist?, by Adam Rose, Time Magazine, 22 January 2010
- Robot passport checker rejects Asian man's photo for having his eyes closed, James Titcomb, The Telegraph, 7 December 2016
- Google Photos Tags Two African-Americans As Gorillas Through Facial Recognition Software, by Maggie Zhang, Forbes, 1 July 2015

- An Other-Race Effect for Face Recognition Algorithms, by P J. Phillips, US National Institute of Standards and Technology, 19 August 2009
- HP computers are racist, YouTube video t4DT3tQqgRM by wzamen01, 10 Dec 2009
- HP looking into claim webcams can't see black people, by Mallory Simon, CNN, 24 December 2009
- Face Recognition Performance: Role of Demographic Information, by Brendan F. Klare, IEEE Transactions on Information Forensics and Security, December 2012

KEEP CALM AND GO BANKRUPT

- 'Keep Calm And Rape' T-Shirt Maker Shutters After Harsh Backlash, by Catherine Taibi, Huffington Post, 25th June 2013
- Remixed Messages, by Rob Walker, 1 July 2009
- Original collection of 'Keep Calm And Carry On' posters could be worth £15,000, The Telegraph, 23 February 2012
- Keep Calm and Carry On: Are the parodies still funny?, Tom Heyden, BBC News Magazine, 6 March 2013
- Aussie 'Keep Calm' T-shirts glorify rape, murder, by Asher Moses, The Sydney Morning Herald, 6 March 2013
- Keep Calm And Rape' T-Shirt Maker Shutters After Harsh Backlash, Catherine Taibi, The Huffington Post, 25 June 2013
- The Bad Things that happen when algorithms run online shops, Chris Baraniuk, BBC Future, 20 August 2015
- Man behind 'Carry On' T-shirts says company is 'dead', Jose Pagliery, CNN, 5 March 2013
- Microsoft is deleting its AI chatbot's incredibly racist tweets by Rob Price, Business Insider, 24 March 2016
- Learning from Tay's introduction, Peter Lee, Official Microsoft Blog, 25 March 2016
- IBM's Watson gives proper diagnosis for Japanese leukemia patient, Alfred Ng, New York Daily News, 7 August 2016
- IBM's Watson Memorized the Entire 'Urban Dictionary,' Then His Overlords Had to Delete It, Alexis C. Madrigal, The Atlantic, 10 Jan 2013

- Prank leaves Justin Bieber facing tour of North Korea, Daniel Emery, BBC News, 5 July 2010

THE MAKING OF A FLY

- Do retailers have to honour pricing mistakes? By Nicole Blackmore, The Telegraph, 29 Jan 2014
- 'I spot and exploit pricing errors for a living', by Ruth Caven, The Telegraph, 12 Dec 2014
- IBM customers buy $1 laptops in site snafu, CNET, 19 January 2000
- Ashford.com flaw allows 'free' purchases, Jeff Pelline, CNet, 2 January 2012
- Screwfix.com price glitch reduces all items to £34.99, by Nicole Blackmore, The Telegraph, 24 January 2014
- How A Book About Flies Came To Be Priced $24 Million On Amazon, Olivia Solon, Wired, 27 April 2011
- Algorithms Gone Wild: 3 Cases of Computers We Trusted Too Much, Muneeza Iqbal, AOL, 13 March 2013
- Bill Gates on giving away his fortune - and Mark Zuckerberg's engagement? by Jemima Kiss, The Guardian, 13 June 2011
- Amazon's $23 million book - algorithms gone wild, Andy Smith, ZDNet, 27 April 2011
- Amazon sellers hit by nightmare before Christmas as glitch cuts prices to 1p, Rupert Neate, The Guardian, 14 December 2014
- IBM customers buy $1 laptops in site snafu, Jeff Bakalar, CNet, 19 January 2000
- Derry firm Repricer Express sorry for Amazon 1p glitch, BBC News, 15 December 2014
- Error hands out $5 fares on United, by John Schmeltzer, Chicago Tribune, 15 May 2002
- United Airlines to honour tickets issued for $0 in glitch, BBC News, 14 September 2013
- Apple given until this afternoon to address pricing error, The China Post News, 27 July 2010
- Apple to deliver cut-price computers to Taiwan after error,

AFP, 28 July 2010

- Website pricing mistake costs Zappos.com $1.6 million, The Las Vegas Sun, 23 May 2010
- Pricing error costs Zappos $1.6 Million, by Josh Smith, AOL. com, 24 May 2010

PANIC AGGREGATOR

- What caused the pound's flash crash?, by Rob Davies, The Guardian, 7 October 2016
- Citi trader deepened October's pound 'flash crash', by Katie Martin and Caroline Binham, Financial Times, 7 December 2016
- Flash Crash of the Pound Baffles Traders With Algorithms Being Blamed, by Netty Idayu Ismail, Bloomberg 7 October 2016
- Testimony Concerning the Severe Market Disruption on May 6, 2010, by Mary L. Schapiro, U.S. Securities and Exchange Commission, 11 May 2010
- How a stray mouse click choked the NYSE & cost a bank $150K, by John Stokes, Ars Technica, 28 January 2010
- Google mistakes high NHS web traffic for cyber attack, Alice Udale-Smith, Sky News, 01 February 2017
- NHS reply-all meltdown swamped system with half a billion emails, by Gareth Corfield, The Register, 31 January 2017
- History's biggest 'fat-finger' trading errors, by Ebony Bowden, The New Daily, 2 October 2014
- Navinder Singh Sarao part 1: reclusive trader or criminal mastermind?, by: Philip Stafford, Lindsay Fortado and Jane Croft, 17 August 2015
- D2MX Pty Ltd pays $120,000 infringement notice penalty, 15-376MR, Australian Securities and Investment Commission, 10 December 2015.
- D2MX Pty Ltd pays 110000 dollar infringement notice penalty, 14-095MR, Australian Securities and Investment Commission, 6 May 2014

THE MIDAS TOUCH

- Inside Michigan's faulty unemployment system that hit thousands with fraud, by Ryan Felton, The Guardian, 12 February 2016
- Thousands of unemployment cases reviewed; 8% affirmed as fraud, by Darren Cunningham, FOX17 News, 21 September 2015
- Criminalizing the unemployed, by Ryan Felton, Detroit Metro Times, 1 July 2015
- Suit settled over false fraud claims against Michigan's jobless, by Paul Egan, Detroit Free Press, 2 February 2017
- Suit filed against state fraud detection vendor, by Paul Egan, Detroit Free Press, 2 March 2017
- Claimants in jobless insurance nightmare pledge: 'Never again.', Paul Egan, Detroit Free Press, 29 January 2017

ROBO-DEBT

- Centrelink's automated debt raising and recovery system, Report by the Acting Commonwealth Ombudsman, Richard Glenn, under the Ombudsman Act 1976
- Call to suspend Centrelink system after single mother receives $24,000 debt notice, by Christopher Knaus and Gareth Hutchens, The Guardian, 27 December 2016
- Centrelink criticised for claiming war widow owed $18,000 after administrative error, by Paul Farrell and Christopher Knaus, The Guardian, 20 April 2017
- Centrelink officer says only a fraction of debts in welfare crackdown are genuine, by Christopher Knaus, The Guardian, 23 December 2016
- Centrelink inquiry told 'income averaging' creating incorrect welfare debts, by Christopher Knaus, The Guardian, 5 April 2017
- Centrelink debt notices based on 'idiotic' faith in big data, IT expert says, Christopher Knaus, 29 December 2016
- Debts As Little As $20 Were Referred To External Collectors

By Centrelink, by Alice Workman, Buzzfeed News, 22 May 2017

- Centrelink to expand its robo-debt program, Sky News, 17 May 2017
- Centrelink targeting $980m from data matching expansion, by Allie Coyne, IT News/Next Media, 19 May 2017
- Fears Centrelink online glitch may send welfare recipients to debt collectors, by Christopher Knaus, The Guardian, 19 December 2016
- Net to Snag Deadbeats Also Snares Innocent, by Megan Garvey, Los Angeles Times, 12 April 1998

THE GRAND RAPIDS MASSACRE

- Christmas and New Year as risk factors for death., by David Phillips, Social Science and Medicine, 7 October 2010
- A deadly computer glitch, Battle Creek Enquirer, 9 January 2003
- The Odd Truth, by Brian Bernbaum, CBS News, 9 January 2003
- Hospital Revives Its "Dead" Patients, by Larry Barrett, Baseline Magazine, 10 February 2003
- System failure behind latest blue cross woes, by Joel Brown, ABC11 WTVD Eyewitness News, 14 January 2016
- Blue Cross customers fume as insurer scrambles to fix ACA enrollment errors, by John Murawski, The Charlotte Observer, 15 January 2016
- Inmates mistakenly released due to software glitch, by KXAN-TV/Associated Press, 19 June 2014
- "Jailhouse rocked:" 25 suspects freed due to computer glitch, by CBS News, 20 June 2014
- Inmates Freed By DPD Computer Glitch Suspects In New Crime by Andrea Lucia, CBS DFW, 19 June 2014

POLICE E-MAIL

- Computer glitch leaves California's neediest Medicare recipients without benefits in 18 counties, Legal Aid Society of San Mateo County, 26 February 2007
- Medicare clients sue state over computer flub, by Beth Winegarner on February 27, 2007
- Lawsuit: Glitch dropped seniors from Medicare, by Michael Manekin, East Bay Times, 27 February 2007
- Computer glitch affects 45K welfare & food stamp recipients, by Melanie Payne, News-Press, 5 November 2016
- Food stamp glitch put 27K in peril, by Melanie Payne, News-Press, 13 March 2014
- Coding error behind missing child protection reports in Qld, by Paris Cowan, ITNews Australia, 20 October 2015
- Qld Education uncovers 270 extra lost child abuse reports, by Paris Cowan, ITNews Australia, 25 August 2015
- OneSchool – Investigation into the 2015 failure of the One-School Student Protection Module, Queensland Department of Education and Training, 16 October 2015
- Glitch causes Florida Abuse Hotline failure to pass on alerts to law enforcement, by Valerie Boey, FOX 35 Orlando, 4 May 2017

GIRLS, ALCOHOL, COCAINE AND WHATEVER

- Glitch hits Visa users with more than $23 quadrillion charge, by Jason Kessler, CNN, 15 July 2009
- Uber says Philly woman's $28,600 authorization hold was a computer glitch by Ben Hooper, UPI, 21 December 2016
- Uber customer in Philly gets surprise charge of $28,000, by Jason Laughlin, The Philadelphia Inquirer, 20 December 2016
- PayPal accidentally credits man $92 quadrillion, by Sho Wills, CNN, July 17, 2013
- Bank glitch makes businessman a billionaire — for five hours, by Keith W. Kohn, Orlando Sentinel, 27 March 2010
- If You Were Billionaire for Five Hours, by Robert Frank, The

Wall Street Journal, 29 Mar 2010
- First Chicago's Big Goof Has Customers A Bit Unbalanced, by John Schmeltzer, 18 May 1996
- $2 million Goulburn fraudster Luke Brett Moore found guilty, The Sydney Morning Herald, 25 February 2015
- The bank lent me $2m so I spent it on strippers and cars, BBC Magazine, 14 December 2016
- Bank error millionaire walks free, by Bernard Lagan, The Times, 3 December 2016
- Woman accidentally given $4.6M by bank, spends most of it on 'luxury' items, by Emanuela Campanella, Global News Canada, 5 May 2016
- Christine Lee allegedly moved $5000 a day into secret accounts to take advantage of a Westpac glitch, News.com.au, 7 May 2016
- Christine Jia Xin Lee's explanation for $4.6 million Westpac overdraft, by Rachel Olding, The Sydney Morning Herald, 22 May 2016
- Australian court bails student who 'spent bank error millions', BBC News, 5 May 2016

THE NORTHUMBRIAN COFFEE PARTY

- Issue Alert - Upcoming CPS Reprocessing of Records with Questionable Income Earned from Work Values, Federal Student Aid Office announcement, 18 July 2014
- Even the feds screw up FAFSA: Online glitch affects thousands, by Claudia Rowe, Seattle Times Education Lab, 22 July 2014
- Stray Decimal Points Put Thousands of Students' Financial Aid in Jeopardy, by David Ludwig, The Atlantic, 23 July 2014
- Bankrupt cancer survivor gets shock: $300 loan balloons into $40,000 debt in 2 years, by Aimee Green, The Oregonian, 3 May 2016
- Misplaced decimal point: Woman owed $400, not $40,000, company says, by Aimee Green, The Oregonian, 6 May 2016
- Mum charged £34,000 for hiring a car for three days in firm's

IT glitch slams Santander for the error, Mirror.co.uk, 13 April 2016

- O2 phone bill 'left couple penniless after decimal point blunder saw their account drained of cash', by James Connell and Dave Rudge, The Mirror, 13 February 2016
- Dropped decimal plays havoc with hotel charges, by Russ Bynum, Associated Press/The Gadsden Times, 2 November 2002
- Glitch Drops Decimal From Holiday Inn Bills, Los Angeles Times, 2 November 2002
- 9000 Amsterdammers krijgen miljoenen door fout, Echt Amsterdams Nieuws, 13 December 2013
- Amsterdam council calls for return of benefits after paying 100 times too much, by Peter Cluskey, The Irish Times, 15 January 2014
- Miss Universe pageant snafu is deja vu, by Mike Stoben, Toronto Sun, 21 December 2015
- Wrong 'Miss Universe Canada' Crowned in Pageant, by Erica Ho, Time, 30 May 2013
- Northumbria University 'life-threatening' caffeine test fine, BBC News, 25 January 2017

ROUNDING UP THE PARLIAMENT

- Fremont Cafe Charging Too Much Sales Tax, by Chris Chmura, Christine Roher and Joe Rojas, NBC Bay Area, 16 March 2017
- Beware lessons of history when dealing with quirky indices, by James Mackintosh, Financial Times, 24 August 2015
- New twist in water billing mess: class action lawsuit, by Alexa Talamo, Shreveport Times/USA Today, 3 April 2017
- Ofcom to examine BT over-charging claims, by Miles Brignall, The Guardian, 28 June 2013
- Millions overcharged because of 'weak' gas, by Jessica Winch, The Telegraph, 24 June 2013
- SEC Charges AXA Rosenberg Entities for Concealing Error in Quantitative Investment Model, Securities and Exchange

Commission Press Release 2011-37, 3 February 2011
- Risks to the public in computers and related systems, by Peter G. Neurnann, ACM SIGSOFT Software Engineering Notes, vol. 17, No. 3, July 1992, ISSN:0163-5948

UNICODE OF DEATH

- Prank crashes iPhones with rainbow emoji messages, Samuel Gibbs, The Guardian, 18 January 2017
- Receiving this rainbow emoji will crash your iPhone, by Liam Tung, ZDNet, 19 January 2017
- A Simple Message Can Crash Skype So Badly You Need to Reinstall It, by Jamie Condliffe, Gizmodo, 3 June 2015
- These 8 characters crash Skype, and once they're in your chat history, the app can't start, by Emil Protalinski, 2 June 2015
- iOS bug lets anyone crash your iPhone with a text message, by Samuel Gibbs, The Guardian, 27 May 2015
- Rendering bug crashes OS X, iOS apps with string of Arabic characters, by Andrew Cunningham and Dan Goodin, 29 August 2013
- Anatomy of a killer bug: How just 5 characters can murder iPhone, Mac apps, by Chris Williams, The Register, 4 September 2013

THAT '70S IPHONE

- Changing your iPhone date to 1 Jan 1970 will not make it retro - it just breaks, by Madhumita Murgia and James Titcomb, The Telegraph, 17 February 2016
- iPhone owners receive ghost emails from January 1, 1970, by James Titcomb, The Telegraph, 7 March 2016
- December 31, 1969, Paypal Community Forum
- This Is Why Facebook Thinks You Have 46-Year Friendships, Eliana Dockterman, Time Magazine, 01 January 2016
- New Threat Can Auto-Brick Apple Devices, Brian Krebs, Krebs On Security, 12 April 2016

FEBRUARY 2038

- Woman, 105, invited to preschool, United Press International, 15 November 2012
- Ryan: Debt on Track to Hit 800 Percent of GDP; 'CBO Can't Conceive of Any Way' Economy Can Continue Past 2037, by Nicholas Ballasy, CNS News, 6 April 2011

HAVE YOU TURNED YOUR DREAMLINER OFF AND ON AGAIN?

- Lost Radio Contact Leaves Pilots On Their Own, by Linda Geppert, IEEE Spectrum, 1 November 2004
- Sunk by Windows NT, Wired, 24 July 1998
- Shock: East Lancs couple receive £500m electricity bill, by Katie Mercer, Lancashire Telegraph, 23 July 2014
- Airworthiness Directives; The Boeing Company Airplanes, Federal Aviation Administration, document number 2015-10066, 1 May 2015
- US aviation authority: Boeing 787 bug could cause 'loss of control', by Samuel Gibbs, The Guardian, 1 May 2015
- To keep a Boeing Dreamliner flying, reboot once every 248 days, by Edgar Alvarez, Endgaget, 5 January 2015
- Software Problem Led to System Failure at Dhahran, Saudi Arabia, Report to the Chairman, Subcommittee on Investigations and Oversight, Committee on Science, Space, and Technology, House of Representatives, Patriot missile defense, by the United States General Accounting Office, February 1992

FREE MONEY SATURDAY

- Computer Glitch Leads To Brawl At Wauwatosa Kmart, WISN Channel 12 Milwaukee, 27 November 2007
- Administrative Proceeding File No. 3-15570 In the Matter of Knight Capital Americas LLC, U.S. Securities and Exchange Commission, 16 October 2013
- Everything You Need to Know About the Knight Capital

Meltdown, by Matt Koppenheffer, The Motley Fool, 14 September 2012

- Joyce Leaving Knight After Steering Firm From Meltdown to Merger, by Sam Mamudi, Bloomberg, 3 July 2013

MR TEST

- Administrative Proceeding File No. 3-15570, US Securities and Exchange Commission, 16 October 2013
- TSA: Computer glitch led to Atlanta airport scare, CNN, 21 April 2006
- Administrative Proceeding File No. 3-17338, US Securities and Exchange Commission, 12 July 2016
- SEC: Citigroup Provided Incomplete Blue Sheet Data for 15 Years, press release 2016-138, US Securities and Exchange Commission, 12 July 2016
- The Role of Software in Recent Catastrophic Accidents, W. Eric Wong, Vidroha Debroy, and Andrew Restrepo, Department of Computer Science University of Texas at Dallas, 2009
- When Does a Test End?, by James Bach, 5 January 2011
- Top Cop Offers "Mea Culpa" to Elderly Couple for 50 Raids, by Jennifer Millman, NBC Channel 4 New York, 19 March 2010
- Computer glitch prompts 50 raids on elderly couple's home, by Dan Goodin, The Register, 19 March 2010
- It's Really Hard to Fill in a Web Form When Your Name Is Mr. Sample, by Patrick McGroarty, The Wall Street Journal, 14 February 2017

FIVE BLANKS HIT THE TARGET

- That "zombie apocalypse" warning in Montana? It was fake, by Laura Zuckerman, Reuters, 12 February 2013
- Police say Mont. TV zombie hoax likely linked to others, by Michael Beall, USA Today, 13 February 2013
- 'Dead bodies are rising from their graves': Hackers use emergency alert system to warn of zombie apocalypse, National

Post/Associated Press, 11 February 2013

- Man's car warns of air raid over London, by Lester Haines, The Register, 25 May 2012
- Digital Alert Systems DASDEC and Monroe Electronics R189 One-Net firmware exposes private root SSH key, CERT, 26 Jun 2013
- Radio stations that ignored major vulnerability start playing anti-Trump song, by Sam Machkovech, Ars Technica, 2 February 2017
- DDoS attack that disrupted internet was largest of its kind in history, experts say, by Nicky Woolf, The Guardian, 26 October 2016
- These 60 dumb passwords can hijack over 500,000 IoT devices into the Mirai botnet, by Graham Cluley, 10 October 2016
- Hard-coded password exposes up to 46,000 video surveillance DVRs to hacking, By Lucian Constantin, CSO/IDG News, 17 February 2016
- Lenovo blunder means '12345678' used as password for default file sharing app, by Jason Murdock, V3, 27 January 2016
- 5-year-old boy hacks dad's Xbox account, Doug Gross, CNN, 4 April 2014
- Security Researcher Acknowledgments for Microsoft Online Services, Microsoft, March 2014

ACKNOWLEDGMENTS

Humans vs Computers would not have been possible without the hard work and incredible support of many people.

Nikola Korac drew all the amazing illustrations that brought this book to life, and Mary White fixed my broken writing and made this book much easier to read.

I owe an enormous debt of gratitude to friends and colleagues who reviewed early versions of this book, and whose harsh criticism and encouragement helped me turn a five page draft into two hundred pages of lively stories. Thank you Alan Richardson, Aleksandar Simovic, Bas Vodde, Christian Hassa, David de Florinier, Dan North, Dejan Dimic, Edwin Dando, Elisabeth Hendrickson, Gordon Weir, James Shore, Jeff Patton, Jeffrey Davidson, Jeffrey Fredrick, Jez Humble, Kent McDonald, Kevlin Henney, Lisa Crispin, Marcus Hammarberg, Matt Wynne, Michael Bolton, Sigurdur Birgisson and Slobodan Stojanovic.

Finally, I would like to thank my business partners from Neuri Consulting, David Evans, Tom Roden and Ben Williams, for their support in getting this project finished, but also years of incredibly valuable discussions and thought provoking ideas.

CPSIA information can be obtained
at www.ICGtesting.com
Printed in the USA
BVOW05*1908310817
493687BV00009B/19/P